The Little
Orange
Handbook
Holland for
Newcomers

Port of Rotterdam

Contents

Living in the Netherlands

Your First Steps

Working in the Netherlands

Money Matters

A place to stay

Education

Getting around

Introduction

Dear reader,

Welcome to *The Little Orange Handbook*! This handy guide to life in the Netherlands provides you with practical tips and hints for living here as well as a compact cultural, historical and economic background on Dutch society and its people's mentality. Just take a quick peek at the table of contents for a first impression of the highly useful stuff waiting for you to explore.

Whether they are expats or foreign students, migrants usually concentrate on the cities – and most Dutch cities are quite attractive indeed. In their historical centers, a rich cultural life flourishes and there are attractions for all tastes and wallets. Many Dutch urbanites are cosmopolitan people with liberal worldviews and sometimes rather unconventional lifestyles, who find themselves rubbing shoulders with others who have more limited views on modern society. And often just 40 kilometers separate these cities from insular villages with strict religious traditions and other forms of conservatism.

Speaking of the countryside; away from cities and highways, the Netherlands has quite a lot to offer in the field of charming scenery and natural beauty, with quiet country roads and wide panoramas in which water is the dominant factor.

Staying in the Netherlands longer than the average tourist would, will make you aware of the pros and cons of living here. On the plus-side, most visitors experience society as being relaxed and open; transparent, and welcoming to new ideas and new people. There is great political and personal autonomy in the Netherlands, with freedom of press, religion and opinion. The Dutch make ample use of this freedom, as you will certainly find after learning the language. Keeping Dutch directness in mind, you will inevitably also hear less pleasant ideas and some extreme opinions, but it is up to you whether you want to go into debate over them or not. Still, whatever your personal lifestyle or your preferences regarding religion, sexuality, politics, etcetera, are; in the Netherlands you can live in accordance with them – provided you respect other people's choices as well…

Other plusses when it comes to life here are the excellent quality of health care and education, both of which rank very highly in world statistics. This book will inform you about some of the particularities when it comes to how it all works, keeping in mind that general standards are very high. Likewise, the country is experienced as child-friendly: children are both loved and taken seriously and numerous are the venues in which tomorrow's citizens can enjoy themselves and develop their skills. Think of museums and theaters, but also of fun parks and child-friendly restaurants.

Not just for children, the Dutch sports scene is also very diverse. Thousands of sports clubs are active, most of which have excellent facilities. Sports facilities, both indoors and outdoors, are to be found everywhere, and in this country known for its plentiful water, all kinds of water sports are popular and well-facilitated. Sports clubs usually also welcome people from 'outside' – even those who do not yet speak the local language – so membership may be a good way to make new friends.

Moreover, life here leaves you time to enjoy it all. The Dutch are a hardworking lot, but they also highly value leisure time. Official workweeks for employees are less than 40 hours, but of course the self-employed and people in leading positions make longer hours. Even so, they enjoy several weeks of holidays and succeed in spending most evenings and weekends with their loved ones. 'Quality time' is not a hot topic here, but Dutch society is certainly not '24/7', and people from more hectic economies can initially be annoyed by this – though most of them find themselves adjusting 'surprisingly' well to a life less stressful.

Less favorable comments on life in the Netherlands usually remark on the many rules and regulations – written but also unwritten ones. Other complaints concern the individualism of the Dutch: the downside of personal freedom is that people may leave you to your own devices. True friendship is a long-term thing in Dutch culture, involving a slow approach with increasingly personal conversation. The Dutch prefer their friends to share certain basic ideas on life and lifestyle, so people from outside need to 'work their way in'. Speaking Dutch will obviously help, but there is an obstacle here too: just about all Dutch people speak English and they almost automatically switch to it as soon as they hear you slowly stumble your way through Dutch. This may be good for fast understanding but not for improving your language skills! Just be 'blunt', and ask them – in Dutch – to speak Dutch.

Quite a few visitors comment on old-fashioned attitudes regarding male-female role patterns: most Dutch women are strong, independent and quite successful, but certain economic and cultural factors may hold them down, obviously a matter under debate.

A final criticism is that the Dutch tend to be rather money-oriented. Even though they may be less thrifty than before, price and 'usefulness' are still important factors in any decision, while more romantic notions such as esthetics, style or fashionability come second.

Overall, the Netherlands is a good place to be, and this book will help you settle in, whether you are an expat, an international student, a love immigrant or any other kind of long-term visitor. Let me conclude by saying: welcome to the Netherlands!

Now before going into detail, a look at Dutch history at large will create the right context and background to help you understand the facts to follow.

You will see how certain contemporary social and cultural idiosyncrasies of the Netherlands stem from developments that took place long ago.

Jacob Vossestein

Jacob Vossestein was an intercultural trainer for over 30 years and is author of the bestselling book *Dealing with the Dutch*

About the
Netherlands

Years of History

200,000 BC The first site to generate human remains: a homo erectus camp. For dinner they had dwarf rhino

120,000 BC Neanderthals

5300 BC The first agricultural settlement in southern Netherlands

3500 BC Era of the people that constructed the dolmens (hunebedden)

2200 BC Stone starts being replaced by copper and later bronze

700 BC Start of the Iron Age

57 BC–402 AD The Romans conquer the country. The Rhine becomes their border. Cities: Nijmegen, Voorburg

400–800 After the fall of the Roman Empire, the Frisian create their own kingdom north of the Rhine. It shares a border with the large Frankish empire, which in the end comprises the entire territory of the current country of the Netherlands. Conversion to Christianity

800–1000 Invasions of the Normans. Creation of independent counties and duchies, which lay at the basis of most of the current provinces

1220 Dordrecht is the first city north of the Meuse and the Rhine to acquire city rights. Ultimately, these are awarded to many cities in the Netherlands

1421 Saint Elisabeth Flood. Creation of the Biesbosch

1396–1467 Philip the Good, Duke of Burgundy, unites most of the counties and duchies of the Netherlands under his reign

1477 Great privilege. The cities, nobility and clergy of the Netherlands recognize Mary of Burgundy,

Dolmens (Hunebedden)

The Romans conquer the country

William of Orange is shot to death

Philip II

granddaughter of Philip the Good, as their Duchess if she honors their rights and privileges. This boils down to her having to rule the area in collaboration with them. Comparable to England's Magna Charta. Predecessor to the Constitution

1568 Battle of Heiligerlee, and the start of the 80-Year War and uprising against Philip II of Spain, Mary's heir. This uprising is in protest against the loss of privileges and rights, as well as against the persecution of the Protestants. The revolt is led by William of Orange

1579 Union of Utrecht

1584 William of Orange is shot to death by a terrorist contracted by Philip II

1602 Establishment of the United East India Company, one of the earliest companies that is financed by means of shares and, for more than a century, by far the largest multinational in the world. Start of the Golden Age

1607 Twelve-Year Truce between Spain and the insurgents. Spain recognizes the independence of the Republic of Seven United Provinces or Seven United Netherlands, which had already been proclaimed by the insurgents in 1588

1648 Definitive peace with Spain

1779 The Republic of Seven United Netherlands recognizes the United States. This leads to the start of a war with England

1780 John Adams is the first representative of the United States in the Netherlands

1795 Towards the end of the 18th century, the century of decline, a French army occupies the Netherlands. The federal and feudal Republic of Seven United Netherlands becomes the Batavian

Republic: a united state, with modern legislation and a modern government

1806 Napoleon appoints his brother Louis King of Holland

1810 Napoleon annexes the Kingdom of Holland

1813 Revolt against the rule of Napoleon. William I is declared sovereign ruler and then King in 1815. The north and south Netherlands are united. The French reforms are maintained

1830 Revolt in Brussels. Belgium secedes

1839 First railroad tracks are laid, between Amsterdam and Haarlem

1848 New constitution. From now on, the ministers are accountable to a directly elected parliament. The King is inviolable

1866 Nieuwe Waterweg is created. This connects Rotterdam with the sea, allowing it to become the largest harbor in Europe

1914–1918 The Netherlands remains neutral during the First World War

1917 Introduction of universal suffrage for men – two years later, for women. The Netherlands becomes a democracy. A government is created in which Christian politicians dominate. Christian politicians remain in all Dutch cabinets until 1993

1919 Foundation Royal Dutch Airlines (Koninklijke Luchtvaart Maatschappij, KLM), based from the home airport of Schiphol near Amsterdam

---

KLM is the oldest national airline in the world

1940–1945 German occupation

1948 The Netherlands joins NATO

1949 The Netherlands recognizes Indonesia's independence, proclaimed by the country itself in 1945

First railroad 1839

German Occupation 1940-1945

1951 Start of the boom and a period of quick economic growth that goes on until the 1970s. The Netherlands is a founding member of the European Coal and Steel Community

1953 North Sea Flood. As disastrous as the Saint Elisabeth Flood

1954 Decision to implement the Delta Plan, aimed at forever avoiding another disaster such as the one in 1953

1957 The Netherlands is a founding member of the Euro market, precursor of the European Union

1963 The Netherlands grants New Guinea to Indonesia

1973 First energy crisis, followed by a recession

1975 Surinam becomes independent

1979 Second energy crisis, followed by the economic crisis of the '80s

1993 For the first time since 1917, a cabinet is formed without Christian politicians, in which liberals and social-democrats work together. Era of an economic boom, stimulated by the ICT market

1995 Blood bath in Srbrenica: Serbian militia slaughter 6,000 Muslim men in Bosnia, in an area that should have been under the protection of Dutch UN troops

2002 Murder of populist Pim Fortuyn. This constitutes the second time that a Dutch politician is shot to death. The first was William of Orange

2008 Due to the credit crisis, the Dutch government has to save the country's largest banks – ABN Amro and ING – with the help of heavy financial injections. ABN Amro is nationalized. A few years later, also the SNS Bank is nationalized. The housing market starts to collapse. Increasing unemployment. Modest recovery only starts in 2014/2015.

1953 North Sea Flood

1973 Energy crisis

The
Netherlands
in a
Nutshell

The Dutch Political System

It took a while for the various peoples of Europe to rid themselves of their absolute monarchs, but eventually also the Dutch managed to make the Netherlands a constitutional monarchy. In a constitutional monarchy, the constitution determines how the powers are divided between the monarch and the other institutions of the government.

The person of the king is inviolable. The ministers are responsible for everything he does or says. This creates a delicate situation; the King, the Queen and their princesses cannot make any public statements without consulting with the Prime Minister first.

The Cabinet

If you have been following Dutch politics for a while, you may have noticed that the number of ministers tends to change from one cabinet to the next. The reasons for this vary. It could be due to the introduction of a new post that is considered sufficiently important under the current circumstances to warrant its own minister. Or it could be in order to ensure that the coalition partners feel proportionately represented in Parliament.

The Parliament

The Netherlands has a representative democracy, with proportional representation. Its Parliament (*Staten Generaal*) is made up of two chambers: the Upper House (*Eerste Kamer*), whose 75 members are elected by the members of the States-Provincial; and the Lower House (*Tweede Kamer,* or Second Chamber), whose 150 members are elected directly by the people.

The elections for the Second Chamber and the Upper House do not take place simultaneously; consequently, a government can have a majority in the Second Chamber, without having one in the First.

The Provincial States

The provinces, of which there are 12, each have their own government, which consists of three bodies: the States-Provincial (Provinciale Staten), the Provincial Executive (Gedeputeerde Staten) and the King's Commissioner (Commissaris van de Koning). The Provincial Executive is charged with the overall management of the province, while the States-Provincial – sometimes referred to as the States General, but that is confusing as there is also a States General of the Netherlands, which is the parliament – is the provincial parliament. It is elected every four years in direct elections, largely from the same political parties as the national elections. Once the Provincial States have been elected, they elect the members of the Upper House within three months.

The King's Commissioner presides over the States-Provincial and the Provincial Executive.

Municipal Councils

Every four years, the inhabitants of the Dutch cities and towns vote for their municipal council. The smallest councils have nine members, the largest, 45. The municipal councils occupy themselves with social services, health care, traffic, public schooling, housing, etc.

The Political Parties

There are ten sizeable parties that have been around for a reasonable period of time, varying from 1918 (the SGP, or Reformed Political Party), to 2006 (the PVV, or Party for Freedom). However, there are several more parties that have sprung up over recent years, as well as parties that cannot be found in the national government, but that can be found in municipal or provincial governments.

Traditionally, the three largest are the PvdA (or Labor Party), a social democratic party that has its roots in the trade union movement; the CDA (Christian Democrats), a merger of three confessional parties that bases its ideas on religious principles; and the VVD, a liberal party. Two other parties that sometimes rise to the top three are the the SP (Socialist Party), and D66, a progressive liberal party that was founded in 1966.

The Other Parties

▶ The SGP is part of national folklore. Its constituents are among the most orthodox protestants of the country.

▶ GroenLinks started out as a merger of several parties that represented a combination of greens, pacifists and communists, and is best summarized as leftist-liberal.

▶ The ChristenUnie is a merger between two religious parties.

▶ The Partij voor de Dieren focuses on supporting animal rights, fighting the inhumane treatment of animals in the bio-industry, and creating an ecologically-based policy.

▶ The Party for Freedom (PVV) is a rightist, political party, whose propaganda mainly focuses on leaving the EU and a rejection of Islam. The PVV is quite successful, and some polls put it at the top if interim elections were to be held.

With 450 people per km² the Netherlands has the highest population density in Europe

Forming a Cabinet

Because there are so many political parties in the Netherlands, there are numerous coalition possibilities. Consequently, after the elections, the Lower House appoints a so-called *informateur*, whose task it is to investigate which political parties could be brought together to create a coalition cabinet.

The Netherlands also has Water Boards, which are responsible for flood control and water resources management

Website

▶ Dutch government: www.overheid.nl/english

Voting

Anyone who wants to vote in the Netherlands must be 18 years of age.

If you are an **EU citizen**, you can vote in municipal elections if you are a resident of a particular municipality on the day on which the candidates are nominated. You can vote for the Water Boards if you live in a 'watership'. To vote for the European Parliament you must be an EU citizen, a resident of the Netherlands, and you may not vote in the same election in your home country, nor be disqualified from voting here or in your home country.

As a **Non-EU citizen**, you can vote in municipal elections if you have been a legal resident of the Netherlands for a continuous period of at least five years, and you can vote for Water Boards if you live in a 'watership' and are a legal resident of the Netherlands.

Only **Dutch nationals** may vote in elections for the Lower House of the Parliament and the Provincial States.

As a member of consular or diplomatic staff, you are not allowed to vote in the Netherlands, nor is your spouse/partner or children who are members of your household

---

Finance Minister Jeroen Dijsselbloem

The Royal Family

Thanks, in great part, to Lady Diana, and now Princess William and Princess Kate, the British Royal Family is closing the light-years-wide gap between the British Royal Family and the public. The Dutch Royal Family, however, is far ahead of them. Queen Wilhelmina, seen as the matriarch of the Netherlands, was loved by the people, politicians and the army, and esteemed by political adversaries. Also her daughter, Queen Juliana, was seen as a kindhearted personality whom people looked up to but loved at the same time. Queen Beatrix, though somewhat more formal, was always greatly respected, and King Willem-Alexander is not only warm, but also youthful and relaxed – more in keeping with modern times and therefore more relatable.

Every now and then, the Netherlands goes through a phase in which calls go up for an abolition of the Royal Family, but the fact remains that the members of this Family are considered so pleasant, politically unobtrusive and inoffensive, as well as warm and modest, that opponents of the Royal Family simply cannot get enough support and the movement fizzles out again.

The Members

The Dutch Royal Family and the 'Royal House' are not the same. Not every member of the Orange Nassau family is a member of the Royal House. The Royal Family is made up of the former Queen and her sisters, their spouses and their children, King Willem-Alexander, his brothers, their spouses and their children and grandchildren. Who becomes a member of the Royal *House* – and therefore could theoretically become the monarch – has been determined by law and consists of the Head of State King Willem-Alexander, his wife Queen Máxima, their children and their spouses and grandchildren, his mother (formerly Queen Beatrix), as well as his brother Prince Constantijn and his wife Princess Laurentien, and his aunt Princess Margriet and her husband Pieter van Vollenhoven.

Members of the Royal House who marry without the official approval of the Parliament, lose the right to succeed to the Throne. When then-Prince Willem-Alexander announced his intention to marry Máxima Zorreguieta of Argentina, there was an iffy moment there, as there was some objection to Máxima's father's possible role in the Argentinean junta from 1976-1983 – but it was decided that though he may have been aware of what was going on, he could not be considered a participant and the couple was given the green light. This has, without a doubt, given the Dutch Royal Family a boost, as Máxima has been well-accepted by the public as an easy-going, respectable, dedicated Queen – and mother of three princesses: Catharina-Amalia (2003), Alexia (2005) and Ariana (2007).

Political Position

The King, together with the ministers, form the government. It was determined in 1848 that the ministers, and not the King, are responsible for acts of government. Laws that have been passed by the Parliament, and Royal Decrees, are signed by both the King (Queen) and the minister in question, lending them the authority of the Head of State but placing the responsibility for them with the minister.

Prince's Day

Every year, on the third Tuesday of September, called *Prinsjesdag*, the King and members of his family ride in the royal Golden Coach from the palace on the Noordeinde to the Binnenhof, where the government is housed. Here the King holds his famous speech, called the *Troonrede*, before the members of the Upper and Lower House, in which the government's policies for the coming year are set out. Prinsjesdag is a popular outing for schools, but also for grown-ups and tourists, who come to The Hague to admire the beauty of the royal procession and taste a bit of the atmosphere of yesteryear.

King Willem-Alexander and Queen Máxima

King's Day

The very first 'regent's day', called Princess Day, was held on August 31, 1895 – in honor of Princess Wilhelmina's fifth birthday. The initiative to organize this was taken by the editor of an Utrecht newspaper, who wanted to celebrate the national unity of the Netherlands. It became a national tradition, with the date following the birthdays of the reigning monarchs: April 30 for Queen Juliana, and now April 27 for King Willem-Alexander. How about Queen Beatrix, you ask? Her birthday is on January 31, and she decided that the chances of a pleasant day of sunshine were considerably greater on her mother's birthday, and left it that way.

Almost every municipality has an 'Orange Association' of die-hard monarchists, who like to arrange a number of festivities that involve a lot of folklore and children's games. Wherever you go, you hear the thump of marching bands and other music. In Amsterdam, people come together to sell their secondhand items on the so-called Free Market (*Vrijmarkt*). This custom has spread across the nation the past 30 years, meaning that you will likely run into your neighbors' kids selling their old toys on that day, which they have spread out on an old rug on the street. They will be flanked by grown-ups who are selling old percolators and other household items for a song. The King and his family visit one municipality on that day – giving the Orange Association the chance to go all out and organize a program of entertainment and fun for the King and his family.

Climate

Boring!

Unfortunately, the Netherlands simply does not have the most exciting of climates. Granted, there are magnificent winter and glorious summer days but, sadly, not very many. This can be very hard to take for those who have not grown up here (and even for those who have!). Many expats comment on how the gray and dreary skies and constant rainfall make it all that much harder to be motivated to get out of bed in the morning and that the only thing that makes it even harder in the winter is that the sun comes up so late. So, what are the facts and how do you get through this?

An unbeatable record was set on March 8, 2013, when it rained a solid 24 hours

Maritime Climate

Thanks to its location right on the North Sea, the Netherlands has a temperate maritime climate with relatively mild winters, mild summers and rain all year round. The Dutch generally feel that it rains a lot here, but statistics say differently. Approximately 7 percent of the time, there is some type of precipitation, such as rain, snow or hail – which translates into 100 minutes of precipitation a day, or 700–800 mm a year. It just *feels* as is its always raining because there is hardly a day on which the meteorologists can guarantee that it *won't* rain. But that doesn't mean it *will*.

Zeeland is the Netherlands' sunniest province

- ▶ Average daytime temperature in winter: 2–6°C
- ▶ Average daytime temperature in summer: 17–20°C
- ▶ The winter of 2015–2016 was the warmest in 300 years, with an average temperature of 9.9 °C
- ▶ Since 1901, dreams of a White Christmas have come true 29 times

- Since 1910, there have been 61 storms with winds between 90 and 122 km/h
- Between now and 2085, the sea level can rise anywhere between 25 and 85 cm

---

The Netherlands has 1,500 hours of sunshine a year

Global Warming

Is there really such a thing as global warming and is the Netherlands suffering the consequences? Who can really say? After all, temperatures have been rising since the end of the last ice age, as have the sea levels. During the ice ages, the sea level was generally 110 meters lower than now. However, during the Cretaceous, it was 220 meters higher. In other words, world temperatures and, unavoidably linked to this, sea levels, fluctuate. In fact, studies show that, over the past 150 years, the rise of the sea level around the Netherlands has shown no acceleration. An unpopular conclusion, perhaps, but maybe we should all just chalk this up to normal fluctuation.

Storms

Which doesn't mean that the Dutch shouldn't protect their land against floods – because if there is one thing history has shown, it is that the Netherlands is rightly worried about them, with the oldest recorded flood taking place in 838. In 1219, one of the most disastrous took place, which affected the provinces of Noord-Holland, Zuid-Holland and Friesland, as well as England and Germany, and which created the Zuiderzee (now known as the IJsselmeer), and the Wadden Sea.

The storm that is most engraved in the collective memories of the Dutch is that of 1953, when 1,800 people in Zeeland drowned and 100,000 people lost their homes. In one single night, 165,000 hectares of land were covered by sea. The storm really delivered a double whammy, however, when on the day after the first floods, the tide came back in again along with strong winds, and took the lives of as many people as it had taken during the first night.

As recently as 2007, a storm caused the sea level to go up to 327 cm higher than NAP (Normaal Amsterdams Peil, or Amsterdam Ordnance Datum; the average summer flood level water in the IJ-River north of Amsterdam. It is used as the reference point for water levels not only in the Netherlands, but also in Finland, Sweden, Norway and Germany).

Looking for something to talk about? Bring up the weather; it is sure to guarantee a conversation that will last as long as you need to fill the time

---

Measures Against Flooding

The country's most famous measure against flooding are the Delta Works, which – though the plans were already on the table before – can be considered the direct consequence of the storm of 1953. They have been created to protect the provinces of Zeeland, Zuid-Holland and Noord-Brabant. Construction started towards the end of the 1960s and it was completed in 1986. It cost approximately 2.5 billion euros and is supposed to reduce the chances of the recurrence of a flood to once every 4,000 years. The American Society of Civil Engineers have declared these works one of the seven wonders of the modern world

Other large-scale measures are the relocation of the dikes in order to broaden the Waal River north of Nijmegen city center, and the Hollandse IJsselkering, meant to protect the lowest part of the Netherlands, which is located 6.76 m below NAP. On average, water levels cause the two 480-ton valves to be lowered into the river three times a year.

The Netherlands is protected by 80,000 kilometers of dikes

Websites
▶ Weather info in English: www.meteovista.com
▶ Weather forecast: www.wunderground.com/nl

Religion

Although modern Dutch society is very secular, and not many Dutch people identify with an organized religion, you will find plenty of churches and other places of worship, and you will have plenty of opportunity to practice your own religion if you wish.

The southern provinces of Brabant and Limburg are predominantly Catholic, and the other provinces are predominantly Protestant. Of the Dutch people who nowadays claim church affiliation, only about 5 percent of the population attends services regularly, and though there are more registered members of the Roman Catholic Church (4.2 million) than of the Protestant Church (1.7 million), only 6.3 percent of the Catholics go to church regularly, while 22 percent of the Protestants do.

With approximately 1 million (practicing) Muslims living in the Netherlands (5.8 percent of the population), Islam has become one of the country's main religions. Mosques have been built in most of the larger cities by communities of immigrants from Turkey, Morocco and Indonesia, and the Dutch public is gradually learning more about Islam – enough to make allowances for colleagues and pupils who are fasting for Ramadan, for example.

Only 13 percent of the Jewish population of the Netherlands, which had been at 140,000, survived the Second World War. This has since grown to sizeable Jewish community of approximately 35,000 members, of which the center is in Amsterdam, though synagogues can also be found in other cities.

- ▶ 42.2% not religious
- ▶ 30% Roman Catholic
- ▶ 20% Protestant
- ▶ 5.8% Muslim
- ▶ 2% other (Hindu, Buddhist, Jehovah's Witness, etc.)

Economy

The Netherlands is in the world's top five in export volume and it ranks in the world's top twenty for GNP, even though it is one of the smallest countries of the world. It owes this favorable ranking, among others, to its advanced transportation infrastructure, the port of Rotterdam (eighth largest seaport in the world in terms of total cargo) and Schiphol Airport (the fifth largest airport in Europe), as well as its advanced telecom infrastructure, extensive (hi-speed) railway network and central geographic location.

Randstad

After Paris, London and Milan, the Randstad (the area including, and between, Amsterdam, The Hague, Rotterdam and Utrecht) is the largest economic urban area in the EU, measured in terms of gross domestic product. This is due to the strong presence of financial and commercial services; which happens to be one of the motors of Dutch economy.

Sectors

The services sector accounts for approximately two-thirds of both the Netherlands' GNP and its work force. Furthermore, the world's largest chemical companies are based here, while the Netherlands is one of Europe's largest suppliers of high-tech goods for both the industrial and the consumer market. It is also Europe's largest producer of natural gas, while Rotterdam imports and refines huge amounts of crude oil that are shipped to the rest of western Europe. Thanks to these offshore installations and refineries, the Netherlands has many activities in the oil and gas industries, including a strong research and development technology and a specialized construction industry.

As for employment: the commercial services sector remains the largest employer in the Netherlands, and has been for several years, closely followed by the health care and manufacturing industries. Also the trade, transport, financial services and information technology sectors are attracting an increasing amount of employees, and science & engineering is showing a constant and steadily increasing need for international and capable workers in areas such as water management, green and renewable energy, as well as logistics.

West Harbor Amsterdam

Holland / The Netherlands

Groningen
Friesland
Drenthe
Noord-Holland
Flevoland
Overijssel
Utrecht
Gelderland
Zuid-Holland
Zeeland
Noord-Brabant
Limburg

Randstad

Amsterdam
The Hague
Utrecht
Rotterdam

Holland or the Netherlands?

Now there's a good question: why is this country sometimes referred to as Holland and sometimes as the Netherlands? The official name of the country you have come to live in is the Netherlands, or 'Low Lands'; a country where 60% of the people live below sea level.

Then why is this country so often referred to as Holland? The answer to this question lies in its history. A few centuries ago, the province of Holland (which included today's North and South Holland provinces) was economically the strongest of all the Dutch provinces, and the one from which virtually all foreign trade originated. Most of the Dutchmen that foreign traders dealt with were Hollanders, literally from Holland. Hence, when talking about the Netherlands, this became the accepted way of referring to the country and its people. Over the years, both names have come to be accepted, although the official name, of course, remains the Netherlands.

Sensitivity

Though it is generally accepted that the Netherlands is referred to as Holland, those who are not from the provinces of North or South Holland do not like to be referred to as Hollanders, or to have their language referred to as *Hollands*. The other Dutch provinces are: Friesland, Groningen, Drenthe, Limburg, Utrecht, Gelderland, Overijssel, Noord-Brabant, Zeeland and Flevoland (the latter came into existence only 28 years ago and consists entirely of reclaimed land).

Randstad

Nowadays, it is of course – long since – no longer the case that the Holland provinces are the most advanced, though most businesses are still located in the provinces of North and South Holland and Utrecht – an area that is commonly referred to as the Randstad. The rest of the Netherlands is just as well-developed and houses many international businesses and expatriates, and the infrastructure (road, rail, water and telephone) is excellent, all across the country.

Some statistics and facts on the Netherlands

► The total land surface area is 33,948 km²/21,218 mi². This excludes all inland and territorial waters wider than 6 meters/20 feet. If all the water surface area is included, the Netherlands has an area of 41,526 km²/25,954 mi²

► The Netherlands' North Sea coastline is longer (642 km) than its border with either Belgium (407 km) or Germany (556 km)

► About 60% of the population lives below sea level

► The highest point in the Netherlands is the Vaalserberg in the province of Limburg; is 321 meters/1,053 feet above sea level

► The lowest point in the country is 6.76 meters/22.18 feet below sea level. It is in the Prince Alexander Polder northeast of Rotterdam (Nieuwerkerk a/d IJssel)

► Head of State: King Willem-Alexander

► Type of state: constitutional monarchy

► Seat of government: The Hague

► Capital: Amsterdam

► Population: 17 million

► 'Non-Western' non-native Dutch: 2.04 million

► 'Western' non-native Dutch: 1.63 million

► Number of households: 7.6 million

► Average life expectancy men born now: 79.2 years, women: 82.9 years

► Average age: 40.1 (gradually increasing: in 1990, it was 36.6)

► Population growth: 120,000 (2013: 48,000)

► Labor force: 7.85 million

► Religion: 4 out of 10 persons profess to being religious

► Most important trade partner: Germany

► Average income: € 35,000 gross

Things the Dutch Invented

1550   **Orange-Colored Carrot** Carrots used to come in all sort or colors; brown, purple, black, yellow and red. The Dutch cross-bred red and yellow carrots to come up with the orange color.

1574   **National Anthem** *Wilhelmus van Nassouwe* is the oldest national anthem in the world.

1606   **Stock Exchange** The Amsterdam stock exchange was the first of its kind in the world, trading in shares from the Dutch East India Company (VOC), which was also the world's first multinational corporation. When politicians today bemoan the lack of drive in the Netherlands, they call for a return to the VOC spirit.

1608   **Telescope** Dutchman Hans Lippershey failed to receive a patent for his invention but a copy of the design was used by Galileo Galilei.

1620   **Submarine** Cornelius Drebbel was the inventor of the first navigable submarine while working for the royal navy. Amazingly, his third prototype could carry 16 passengers and travelled under water from Westminster to Greenwich during a demonstration for Britain's King James 1.

1670   **Microscope** Antonie van Leeuwenhoek became the first man to make and use a real microscope.

1672   **Fire Hose** Talented landscape painter Jan van der Heyden, and his brother Nicolaes, invented the first fire hose and was later put in charge of Amsterdam's firefighting department.

1828   **Chocolate Bar** Amsterdam chemist Casparus van Houten Sr. patented an inexpensive method for pressing the fat from roasted cocoa beans and creating a solid mass that could be pulverized into cocoa powder. This powder became the basis for chocolate products today.

1903 **Electrocardiograph (ECG)** Willem Einthoven was awarded a Nobel Prize for his invention.

1903 **Four-Wheel Drive with Internal Combustion Engine** In 1903, the Dutch car manufacturer Spyker introduced the first four-wheel drive car with an internal combustion engine, the Spyker 60 HP. A revived Spyker Cars still makes luxury cars today. It also bought Saab which then went bankrupt.

1943 **Artificial Kidney** The first artificial kidney was developed by Willem Johan Kolff.

1958 **Speed Camera** Dutch company Gatsometer, founded by the 1950s rally driver Maurice Gatsonides, invented the first speed camera so that Gatsonides could monitor his speed around the corners of a race track.

1979 **Compact Disc** After the compact cassette in 1962, Philips together with Sony came up with the compact disc. Both now defunct of course.

1994 **Bluetooth** Jaap Haartsen invented the wireless communication system Bluetooth.

2005 **Stormproof Umbrella** Gerwin Hoogendoorn became frustrated and invented the stormproof umbrella.

Note: The Dutch think they invented printing but they didn't

Unesco World Heritage

UNESCO Werelderfgoed
Waddenzee

United Nations
Educational, Scientific and
Cultural Organization

UNESCO Werelderfgoed
Stelling van Amsterdam

United Nations
Educational, Scientific and
Cultural Organization

UNESCO Werelderfgoed
Schokland

United Nations
Educational, Scientific and
Cultural Organization

UNESCO Werelderfgoed
Droogmakerij
De Beemster

United Nations
Educational, Scientific and
Cultural Organization

UNESCO Werelderfgoed
Willemstad, Curaçao

United Nations
Educational, Scientific and
Cultural Organization

UNESCO Werelderfgoed
Ir. D.F. Woudagemaal

United Nations
Educational, Scientific and
Cultural Organization

UNESCO Werelderfgoed
Rietveld-Schröderhuis

United Nations
Educational, Scientific and
Cultural Organization

UNESCO Werelderfgoed
Molencomplex Kinderdijk

United Nations
Educational, Scientific and
Cultural Organization

JNESCO Werelderfgoed
Grachtengordel
Amsterdam

United Nations
Educational, Scientific and
Cultural Organization

UNESCO Werelderfgoed
Van Nelle fabriek

United Nations
Educational, Scientific and
Cultural Organization

UNESCO World Heritage Sites

The Netherlands has ten UNESCO World Heritage sites, each of which represents a unique aspect of Dutch history. In the near future, this list will be expanded upon.

1 Van Nelle Factory – 2014

The Van Nelle factory was the tenth item to be added to the Dutch UNESCO World Heritage List. This is sure to be music to the ears of those who fought to avoid its destruction towards the end of the '90s of the previous century. Back in 1923, the then-director of Van Nelle ordered the construction of a 'hyper-modern' factory, which would provide space, light and air for the employees. The factory opened in 1931 and during the next 60 years produced tea, tobacco, coffee, instant pudding and chewing gum. Then, in 1995, production stopped, but luckily a group of investors came along and, in the mid-2000s, its doors opened again and it became a popular location for events and offices.

2 Amsterdam Ring of Canals – 2010

The Amsterdam Ring of Canals – 14 kilometers long and encompassing 80 bridges – is an urban planning, water management and architectural masterpiece. It was constructed around the 17th century – the Golden Age – and accompanied by the construction of narrow merchant's houses. Most of these houses had several storeys and were where the merchants both lived and worked. At first, the houses varied little from each other, with the exception perhaps of their façades – with their stepped, neck and clock gables. Later came the construction of double canal houses and so-called manor houses, though this was reserved, of course, for the very wealthy. The latter houses have now acquired the name 'city palaces' and you can find them in the well-known Gouden Bocht (Golden Bend) of the Herengracht.

3 Willemstad Curaçao – 1997

The inner city of Willemstad has been on the UNESCO
World Heritage list since 1997 and is often referred to as the
'Amsterdam of the western hemisphere'. Here you will find a lot
of authentic Dutch architecture, as well as street names that will
remind you of the city's Dutch heritage, such as the Heerenstraat,
Prinsenstraat and Breedestraat. Yet, the city's architecture is
not all Dutch; it also has Portuguese influences and is, in fact, a
colorful mix of styles. All in all, the typical Caribbean colors have
become predominant.

4 Droogmakerij De Beemster – 1999

This particular World Heritage site is an entire municipality –
with its beautiful, historic church and several museums, as well as
authentic cheese-cover farmhouses, all surrounded by the typical
North-Holland landscape. The best way to explore the town is
on foot or by bicycle, following the route that takes you along the
museums and the farmhouses – with the occasional place to stop
and take a well-deserved rest.

5 Kinderdijk-Elshout Windmills – 1997

There is no better place in the world to admire the
development of water management than in Kinderdijk. Which is
exactly why this site was added to the UNESCO World Heritage
list. It encompasses a large polder area with storage basins,
dikes, pumping stations and mills. It is *the* place to discover how
the Dutch succeeded in laying dry and protecting the land.

There are 1,170 operational windmills in the Netherlands

6 Schokland – 1995

Schokland was the first Dutch monument to be placed on the UNESCO list. Also here you can admire how the fate of the Dutch people is intermingled with that of the country's water. Initially, the island was located in what was then known as the Zuiderzee (now IJsselmeer) and its inhabitants were forced to watch, helplessly, as the wild sea claimed their land. It has since become an elongated strip of land that lies slightly higher than the surrounding polder and that houses several points of interest, including its church, lighthouse keeper's house, and the stones that were deposited there during the Ice Age – as well as other national monuments, archeological dike systems, mounds, and prehistoric sites.

7 Wadden Sea – 2009

Whereas the Dutch and German portion made it onto the UNESCO list in 2009, the Danish part of the Wadden Sea was added in 2014. The three countries aim to work together to protect this area's natural habitat, which is the world's largest system of island, sand and mudflat plates – to a total of approximately 11,500 square kilometers, bringing it in a league with the Great Barrier Reef and the Grand Canyon!

8 Rietveld Schröder House – 2000

From 1923–1924, Gerrit Rietveld worked on the Rietveld Schröder House, whereby he was influenced by the art movement called 'De Stijl' ('The Style', or neoplasticism). He developed it in close collaboration with his client Truus Schröder-Schräder, who wanted it to be a place that was 'free from association' – for instance, the living room is not on the ground floor – which gave Mrs. Schröder a greater sense of freedom. After her death, the Centraal Museum took over its management and arranges exhibitions there, including a permanent exhibition containing some of Rietveld's pieces of furniture.

9 Ir. D.F. Wouda Pumping Station – 1998

During the early 1900s, Friesland was besieged by water problems and in 1913 the decision was made to construct a pumping station near Lemmer. This was carried out by Ir. Dirk Frederik Wouda, head engineer of the Provincial section of the former Ministry of Transport, Public Works and Water Management. The pumping station is operational to this day and is yet another symbol of the Dutch people's daily struggle with water.

10 Defense Line of Amsterdam – 1996

The Defense Line of Amsterdam is made up of 46 forts and batteries, as well as a tremendous amount of sluices and dikes – creating, all in all, a defense line of 135 kilometers. The aim was to protect Amsterdam against both water and invaders and it took approximately 40 years to create. It was finished just before the start of the First World War, though no battles ever took place here after its construction. It is open for visitors in many parts and is also a great place for hiking and cycling.

The Dutch Culture

Gay Parade, Amsterdam

Core Values in Dutch Society

The core values in Dutch society are: freedom, equality and solidarity.

▶ The Netherlands is a democracy. Its inhabitants have a say in who runs the country. It is also a constitutional state. Everyone has the same rights and must adhere to the same rules. Also the government.

▶ Everyone is responsible for their own sustenance. If they are unable to do this – for whichever reason – there is a social safety net.

▶ In order to succeed in the Netherlands you must learn Dutch. Which is why there is an assimilation course and obligation to attend this course.

▶ Everyone has a right to medical care: to this purpose, everyone must take out medical insurance. This insurance will cover most of your medical expenses.

▶ Children between the ages of 5 and 16 must go to school. If they have not graduated at that age, they must continue until the age of 18. (There are three types of high school here, from which you graduate at either age 16, 17 or 18 – provided you complete every year on schedule).

▶ Everyone must pay taxes. The more you earn, the more you pay. The Dutch authorities use this tax money to pay for things that are in everyone's interest – such as roads, medical care, education and safety.

▶ Dutch society – based on humanistic and Judeo-Christian traditions – is open. People are free to say what they think. No one is obligated to live according to any particular philosophy. Discrimination is punishable by law.

▶ People of different religious backgrounds can live together safely here. No one may be made to feel threatened or unsafe because of their religion. You are free to demonstrate your beliefs through jewelry containing religious symbols, headscarves or yarmulkes. Some professions require uniform clothing, such as the army, the police or the courts.

▶ Everyone is free to choose their own lifestyle. It's up to you what type of music you listen to, what type of clothes you wear, what type of work you do, which newspaper you read and what you eat. You can marry whomever you want and declare whichever sexuality you wish. There is of course a limit to all this freedom: you have to be considerate of other people and you may not incite violence.

▶ It is important that you feel at home in the Netherlands, get to know people and participate in society. You can join a sports club, go to a community center, go to university or follow a course. You can even start your own association/club. For instance, for sports – or a union, a political party, or a society for people from your home country.

▶ The right to self-determination means that you can decide what you do with your body. No one may hurt you or even touch you if you don't want this. Even a doctor can only examine you with your permission. The law contains exceptions to this rule, such as in the case of police checks. The right to self-determination includes abortion and euthanasia.

▶ All people are equal – not the same, for everyone is different – but deserving of equal treatment, be they man or woman, gay or 'straight', young or old, and born in the Netherlands or in another country.

▶ Solidarity means that we take each other into account and that we know that others will do the same for us. The Netherlands is one of the richest countries in the world. But the government cannot be expected to do everything. Which is why it is important that people help each other. Many people here do volunteer work. For instance, in a sports club, or at schools. Others take care of someone at home, including offering to share their home with refugees for a while.

The Netherlands has 2,360 kilometers of highway

Through Other Eyes

Many Spaniards are of the opinion that the Netherlands smells of grass, trees and fallen leaves. The Turks think the Dutch should wash their butts and not wipe them. What do other people think of the Dutch?

The Belgians, our southern neighbors, are of the opinion that the Dutch are loud, hyperactive, relatively immodest, and insensitive to hierarchy and authority. And they do not appreciate the 'Orange Madness' that accompanies soccer or skating. They are more positive about their neighbors when it comes to their tolerance, frugality, soberness, and assertiveness, as well as their love for the Royal Family, and their willingness to work hard. And they see the Dutch as entrepreneurial.

Cheese has been made in the Netherlands since 400 AD

The Spaniards do not like the fact that you have to get out your agenda to make an appointment. They feel the Dutch neglect their elderly and are not huge fans of the lunch sandwich. And they notice the stinginess. They are more appreciative, however, of the tolerance, generosity and thoughtfulness of the Dutch as well as of their well-organized roads and train stations…

The French do not appreciate Dutch food at all; the tomatoes are vile and their cheese has the texture of plastic. They also do not approve of the Dutch policy on soft drugs. They think the Dutch language is odd with all those guttural sounds and they find the Dutch miserly. They become more enthusiastic when they discuss the Dutch arts and culture, their multilingualism, their straightforwardness, the flatness of the country, and its order and cleanliness.

The total length of Dutch roadways is 132,397 km. That is four times the circumference of the Earth

---

The English really do not like the (rude) directness of the Dutch. However, they are more focused on the positive side: the easy-go-

King's Day, Amsterdam

ingness of the Dutch, their relaxedness, multilingualism, beautiful women, sincerity, honesty and the relative lack of social classes.

The Hungarians have no complaints. To them, the Netherlands is a wealthy nation with rich people, excellent roads and beautiful gardens.

The Dutch are the tallest people in the world, at 170 cm for women and 184 cm for men

---

The other neighbors, the Germans, are not quite as positive as their Hungarian friends. When asked, they come up with terms such as: loud, arrogant, pushy, stingy, drug users, messy streets, chaotic roads and bad food in the restaurants. On the other hand, they find the Dutch entrepreneurial, welcoming, environmentally engaged, crazy about symmetry, and informal in the workplace, while the Germans enjoy coming here on short vacations, particularly to the Dutch coast.

The Dutch smoke more than 24 billion cigarettes every year

Okay, let's take a look at a few other continents: North America. Negative, according to them: the use of weed, wooden shoes, mayonnaise on fries, nose-picking, lousy customer service and traffic jams.

Positive: easygoing/relaxed, welcoming, multilingual, tolerant, progressive, 'cute', tall and blond, good cheeses, creative, level-headed, direct, weather discussers, generally healthy, good company, while the country is green, full of flowers, flat, with short distances and few debts.

The Russians are the least enthusiastic about the Netherlands. On the positive side is the tolerance, but other than that – to them – the Netherlands is simply part of Germany: bad-mannered, fat inhabitants who eat like pigs and are stingy, loud, arrogant, boring, excessive smokers, wild about anything that's free and lacking in parenting skills. Interestingly, this is exactly how Dutch tourists describe the Russian tourists they come across abroad…

The Japanese – who in this case represent Asia – are of the opinion that the Dutch are rude, uncouth, egocentric, spoiled, undiplomatic and aggressive. On the other hand, they also see the

Dutch as assertive, independent, creative and full of initiative.

Let's just say, wherever you're from, you're bound to be hit by at least a smidgen of culture shock.

Cultural Mistakes You Will Make

There are some things you cannot learn from integration courses. Glaring mistakes you just have to make to confirm that you are a true foreigner in the Netherlands. Here are a few that we have all been guilty of.

- ▶ **You'll be late** Even one minute late is considered rude by Dutch standards. Traffic, getting lost, delays at work, difficulty finding parking, and every other excuse considered acceptable by all other nationalities will not earn you forgiveness. Though you can try to blame it on train delay. And curse the rudeness of NS to have made you late.
- ▶ **You fail to make an appointment** Want grab coffee with your neighbor? Break out your calendar and schedule it 4–6 weeks in advance. Whatever you do, don't just drop by.
- ▶ **You will forget flowers** If invited over to a Dutch person's home, you will be expected to bring a gift. While some more open-minded folks will welcome a bottle of wine or chocolates, it's more common to bring flowers. And not flowers from Albert Heijn either. But wait... Don't go getting a guy flowers, bring beer instead.
- ▶ **You will not offer your colleagues coffee or tea** If you want grab a coffee during the work day, you better check with your entire office first, including janitorial staff and people on the night shift. Call them if necessary. You will be expected to bring back fourteen different orders, because everyone in the office will say yes.
- ▶ **You will decline something without saying thanks** If you do, god forbid, turn down your colleague's offer of coffee or tea, be sure to say "No, thank you" or "Nee, bedankt." Even when declining the receipt at the grocery store, you better include that "Thanks". Otherwise, you might as well spit on their shoes.

▶ **You will not offer your guests tea or coffee** If anyone comes over to your house for any reason, you better be prepared to offer coffee, tea, and some type of biscuit. It doesn't matter if it's the plumber who is there because your sink exploded, or your future mother-in-law: you will be considered rude for not offering.

▶ **You will fail to bring birthday cake to the office** It is your birthday, but you are expected to give everyone else a present – in the form of a piece of cake or pie. You must arrange the cakes, usually *Vlaamse Vlaaien*, next to the coffee machine.

▶ **You will fail to congratulate your colleague on her husband's birthday** You congratulate everyone not only on their own birthday, but on the birthday of anyone who is near and dear to them. Failing to do this is considered insensitive and uninterested.

Nine Things Non-Dutch Children Love About Living in Holland

Pancakes
This is at the top of nearly everyone's list. Dutch *pannenkoeken*, or pancakes, preferably with syrup and icing sugar, possibly banana and chocolate sauce, bacon and apple, shawarma, grilled chicken… you name it, you can have it on a pancake.

Bikes
From about the age of four, Dutch kids can be seen riding their own bicycles, without training wheels, around the neighborhood. Were they born this way? Non-Dutch kids are soon addicted to the freedom a bike allows and – thanks to the cycle paths – as a parent you feel relaxed that your offspring are safe cycling to school or to friends' houses. Not that you will manage to force them into a bike helmet of course. And as soon as they turn 16, they will start muttering about wanting a scooter.

Dutch Pancakes

There are more bicycles than people in the Netherlands: approximately 18 million

Hagelslag and other things on bread

Chocolate sprinkles on your sandwiches – not difficult to see why kids like this, or why becoming a dentist is something you should encourage your children to aim for. *Hagelslag*, chocolate paste, *speculaas* cookies, and *muisjes* – all sweet and delicious on soft, white bread! As an expat mother, your house may be boycotted by your children's friends unless you have *hagelslag* in the cupboard.

Hagelslag

According UNICEF the Netherlands is the best country to grow up in for kids

Schools

No uniforms and almost no homework! If your kids have gone to school in almost any other country other than the Netherlands, attending a Dutch school, once they have tackled the language, is going to be a breeze. The no uniform policy is particularly loved by teenage girls, who grab the opportunity to dress up and perfect their makeup before cycling off to chemistry class.

Amusement parks

The Dutch love them – one of the most famous rollercoaster makers in the world is a Dutch company. Be prepared to hand over a large heap of cash and spend a lot of time waiting in queues… but Walibi, Efteling, Linnaeushof, Duinrell, Drievliet, Slagharen and Hellendoorn, among others, are waiting for you.

Skating

Like with bikes, Dutch kids are forced onto skates as soon as they can walk, so your expat kids will probably have some catching up to do. But if there is a big freeze, there will be no holding them back. Outdoor skating also means great pics to post on Facebook for admiring friends and relations.

One out of three Dutch residents is a member of a sports club

Sports

Forget school sports – in the Netherlands it's all about club competitions, whereby six and seven-year-old fanatical football players and hockey starts will find themselves whisked off to matches all over the place. Hockey clubs, in particular, appeal to teenage girls because they get to dress up in short skirts and have attitude at the same time. And don't forget the parties. Lots of parties.

Birthdays

The egalitarian Dutch custom of ensuring no-one gets left out means your children will soon come to associate every birthday with a little gift, whether or not it is their own birthday. As a parent, you will be driven insane by having to come up with something clever and imaginative to eat which your child can hand out in class on his or her birthday.

Vice

So this is the one they don't talk about – but expat teens are secretly thrilled at the extra layer of cool that living in the sex and drugs-riddled Netherlands gives them among their friends in other places. But parents don't need to worry. Dutch kids have one of the lowest teen pregnancy rates in the world and are much less likely to abuse drugs than their peers in other countries. The UN says so.

Twelve Clues to Under-standing the Dutch Mentality

At first sight, the Dutch appear to be like many other normal Europeans. But those of you who have lived here longer and have worked with the Dutch, will have found dramatic differences. In short, it might be good to know a little more about the Dutch culture. In these paragraphs, you will find a short overview of the twelve principles or values that rule Dutch society, from politics, work, and school, to the most intimate parts of family life.

The first four values come straight from Christianity:

1 **Salvation** Your sacrifices and efforts will be rewarded in the future

2 **Guilt** You are responsible for the good and bad things that are the consequences of your acts

3 **Love thy Neighbor** You should be concerned about the welfare of others

4 **Truth** You should always tell the bare facts

In the first place, the Dutch, just as other people who live in Christian cultures, are strongly oriented towards the future. Progress and innovation are important issues. Secondly, they are always worrying whether they did things right or wrong. The degree of personal responsibility is high. Thirdly, the Dutch feel greatly involved with people who have troubles, or who are suffering – whether close to home or on the other side of the world. This is evident from the country's extensive social security system and its high budget for developmental aid. Fourthly, the Dutch put a lot of stock in the objective truth and the bare facts. They find it more important to tell someone else exactly what they think than to be polite.

The next five values follow from Protestantism:

5 Work
It is good to work

6 Order & Tidiness
You should be well-organized

7 Utility
Everything you do, must have a purpose, you may not waste

8 Reliability
You must do what you promised

9 Moderation
You must exercise self-control, and must not overdo

The Dutch think that it is better to work than to idly sit by. The higher they are on the corporate ladder, the harder they work. They appreciate an organized life that is dictated by the clock and their agenda, and think that a house should be neat and clean. The Netherlands is a relatively clean and well-organized country, in which a lot of big and little rules tell you how to behave. Also abroad, the Dutch are known for their tightness. One thing is certain; they hate waste; of money, time or anything else. Don't be surprised if they ask you what purpose your proposal serves. Couldn't it be done more efficiently, or perhaps effectively? The Dutch are very literal about their agreements and promises; if you agree to do something, then you must actually do it, or they will conclude that you are unreliable. In daily life, the Dutch hate extremes and exaggeration, they applaud self-restraint and frown upon expressing strong emotions. Only under certain conditions (a soccer match, carnival, at a disco), do they ever let it rip.

All this may sound pretty familiar to people from other Christian or Protestant countries. But the difficult part is still to come.

The last three principles are typically Dutch and explain why certain things are done differently here or are found to be different than they are in the surrounding countries.

10 Consensus
You should always try to compromise

The Dutch dislike conflict and aggression, and consistently strive for consensus and harmony, which they refer to affectionately as *gezelligheid*. They devote quite a bit of time to meetings and discussions, in order to make sure that all disagreements have been resolved. Instead of letting the democratic majority rule the minority, they prefer to find a solution that appeals to everyone; a compromise. A compromise that everyone will then stick to, for fear of conflict. This is often referred to as the *poldermodel*. Consequently, the Netherlands has a relatively peaceful, non-violent society, in which strikes end rather quickly in compromise and the police apply a de-escalating approach to handling skirmishes.

11 Equality
You should not think that you are better than anyone else

In the Netherlands, all hierarchy and differences in social status are carefully smoothed over and disguised. It is painful to give direct instructions to someone who is under you, such as your cleaning lady. You can't just say: "Daisy, clean up the kitchen and the bathroom!" To the Dutch, this is a brusque order against which they rebel immediately. Instead, they formulate it as a polite question: "Would you perhaps be willing to do the kitchen and the bathroom today?" It sounds like a suggestion, but to the Dutch, this already feels like giving/receiving an order. The Dutch do not apply politeness towards superiors, but rather reverse politeness towards inferiors. You must, at all cost, avoid the impression that you think you might be superior to the other (even if you are a minister or have won the Nobel prize). It is perfectly easy to manage the Dutch, provided you treat them as equals and disguise every instruction as a friendly request.

The Dutch are allergic to people who toot their own horn; they expect modesty and if you fail to act like a 'normal' person, then you will be mowed down. You are not only not allowed to be openly proud of your achievements, the same applies to being proud of your country and your history. To many Dutch people, nationalism is a cardinal sin. This is not to say that the Dutch are not proud of their country; they just cannot say so openly.

12 Self-Determination I will decide what I do – not my father, boss or government

The Dutch find it more important that people be allowed to make their own choices, than to tell them what to do. Their motto is: everyone should decide for themselves what to do, as long as what they do doesn't interfere with my life. This is the basis for Dutch tolerance: it is not so much that they understand people who think differently, as that they are pragmatic; if you leave me alone, I will leave you alone. This explains why the Dutch tolerate the use of soft drugs, abortion and euthanasia. It does not so much mean that they 'do' it, but rather that they feel that whether or not someone else does, is their personal choice and none of anyone's business. This explains why so many different lifestyles can coexist in such a small country, from extravagant gay people who marry, to black-clad orthodox protestants who go to church three times every Sunday.

Children are not so much raised to respect their elders or general moral principles – but to think for themselves and speak for themselves. Dutch employees are expected to demonstrate a high degree of responsibility and initiative. Do take into account therefore that all Dutch people, be they young or old, have an opinion on everything and want to be heard. After which they will call a meeting, to reach a compromise!

Popular Finger Food

Top 10 yummy (at least, as far as the Dutch are concerned), typical Dutch finger food.

Cubes of cheese or sausage with a piece of pickle or silver-skin onions on a toothpick with a Dutch flag at the end

1

2 Bitterballen

3 Dutch meat balls

4 Deviled eggs

5 Toast with herring, eel and salmon

6 Toast with 'salad'

7 Rye bread with herring and onions

8 Mini cheese souffles

9 Potato salad

10 French bread (with garlic butter)

1 **Cubes of cheese or sausage with a piece of pickle or silver-skin onions on a toothpick with a Dutch flag at the end.** Probably the easiest-to-recognize finger food. Easy to prepare and festive-looking with its little flag.

2 **Bitterballen (deep-fried meat ragout, coated in bread crumbs).** Another classic – and Dutcher than Dutch. Don't forget to serve them with mustard; an essential ingredient to create the authentic 'bitterbal-experience'.

3 **Dutch meat balls.** These are very popular here. Though they are easy to prepare, no two are the same and some families strictly guard their secret family recipe over centuries.

4 **Deviled eggs.** Another party favorite. They look complicated, but are easy to make. Hard-boil eggs, peel them, cut in half, remove the egg yolk. Mix the yolk with grated cheese, sour cream, chives, garlic, ginger syrup, pepper and salt. Scoop back into the halves of egg white and sprinkle with ground paprika.

5 **Toast with herring, eel and salmon.** Also easy to make. Make toast (or use crackers) and cover with either herring, eel or salmon. These go back centuries!

6 Toast with 'salad'. The modern-day version of toast with fish. In this case, you buy egg salad, tuna salad, crab salad, chicken curry salad… and serve it on toast (or crackers).

7 Rye bread with herring and onions. Not hard to prepare: take a slice of rye bread, place herring on top, sprinkle with chopped onion and voilà.

8 Mini cheese souffles. Something you would be hard put to find outside of the Netherlands. Serve with mayonnaise, curry sauce or chili sauce.

9 Potato salad. An excellent dish to serve along with the previous finger foods. You usually place it on the table so that people can serve themselves. Eaten with a fork.

10 French bread (with garlic butter). Another side dish to accompany the finger foods. You can cut it in little round slices and place these on the table, in a basket. Or you can place it on a cutting board with a knife and let your guests do their own slicing. Place a generous dish of garlic butter next to it.

Every year, the Dutch throw away 110 million loaves of bread

Typical Dutch Festivities

Carnival

Carnival, the Dutch either love it or hate it. Those who live *beneden de rivieren* (below the rivers, in other words in Noord-Brabant or Limburg) love it and celebrate it with a passion. Virtually all businesses close (except cafés and restaurants of course) in a three-day celebration of life, spring, beer and friendship. In the provinces *boven de rivieren* (above the rivers), the general attitude towards carnival is one of aloofness – adding to their reputation among the Southerners as a dour and 'un-fun' people – a gray dividing line that, some would say, smacks of a still Protestant-based north and a predominantly Catholic south.

People get dressed up and go from café to café, singing songs, participating in parades and consuming large quantities of beer. There is no need to be afraid of this being a local festivity at which strangers are not accepted: strangers are welcome, and it is a great way to meet new people. Breda, Maastricht and 's-Hertogenbosch are three of the major venues.

April 27: King's (Birth)Day

Although not necessarily known to be royalists, the Dutch are extremely fond of their Royal Family. Throughout history, the Dutch Royal Family has been very popular and the Family's birthdays have been celebrated with enthusiasm.

You can celebrate the King's birthday either by visiting the town or city the King visits on this day – and witness traditional entertainment and games – or you can visit some of the bigger cities. Amsterdam, in particular, goes all out on this day, with a *vrijmarkt*, a free market that fills the streets in the center of Amsterdam with stands run by people age 5 – 105, selling anything and everything. People from all across the world come to Amsterdam. Another option is to visit the traditional *koningsmarkt* (King's Market) of your own town, where the locals sell just about anything for a song, a great opportunity for bargain hunters and antique buffs – but be there early for the best values (6 A.M.)!

Commemorating the Dead: May 4th

More a day of national significance than of festivity, May 4th is initially the day on which the Dutch remember the victims of the

Second World War: soldiers, people in the Resistance and those who died in the concentration camps in Europe as well as in Indonesia. Since 1961, the commemoration has been expanded to include all war victims in the years since the Second World War. Between 8 P.M. and 8:02 P.M., a two-minute silence is observed nationally. People stop whatever they are doing (often pulling their cars over to the side of the road) to remember those who did not make it through the war. Even local radio and television broadcasts are halted. In many municipalities, people come together for short ceremonies, particularly in The Hague, on the Waalsdorpervlakte, and in Amsterdam, on the Dam Square. Flags are hung half-mast throughout the country.

Liberation Day: May 5th

Following the sober day of May 4th, the Dutch celebrate their total liberation from the occupying forces in 1945 (some parts of the Netherlands had been liberated in November 1944) on Liberation Day, May 5th. This day is not celebrated as extensively as it used to be: some businesses and most government offices close (in keeping with the collective labor agreement), but most do not. However, there is always some celebration going on somewhere,

Joyful Dutch civilians and Canadian
soldiers celebrate the liberation

while movies and documentaries about this period on TV provide you with the opportunity to learn a little bit about (recent) Dutch history if you want.

Trick or Treats – Sint Maarten

Increasingly, the trick or treats day of November 11 is being reintroduced. On this day, children (often accompanied by parents) come by your door, carrying lanterns and singing songs such as '*Sint Maarten, Sint Maarten, de koeien hebben staarten, de meisjes hebben rokjes aan, daar komt Sint Martinus aan*' (St. Martin, St. Martin, the cows have tails, the girls wear skirts, there comes St. Martin – who *knows* what the one has to do with the other). This day is a 'treats'-day – no tricks – the treats being anything from tangerines to cookies to candy. The children do not get dressed up for this occasion, either; it is a simple – though friendly and *gezellige* – neighborhood event. In some cities, due to the exposure to other cultures, rather than with Sint Maarten on November 11, children go trick or treating on October 31, Halloween.

The Dutch eat an average of 2 kilos of licorice (drop) a year

---

Sinterklaas / St. Nicholas

December 5th is St. Nicholas's birthday when, according to legend, this 4th-century Saint gave gifts of gold to three poor girls for their dowries (children still receive chocolate coins around this time). As Sinterklaas is considered the patron saint of children, he brings them gifts that are surreptitiously dropped off in a sack on the doorstep of each household on December 5th. (Usually, a neighbor is involved in this process: the parents bring him the sack sometime during the day and he or she promises to drop it on the doorstep and bang on the door. This is the cue for the children to yell 'Sinterklaas!' and run to the door, in hopes of catching the retreating form of Sinterklaas or Zwarte Piet. Instead, they find the sack of gifts and completely fail to notice the happy neighbor, hidden around the corner, having made his or her escape just in time.)

Arrival of Sinterklaas

Somewhere mid-November, Sinterklaas makes his official entry into the Netherlands, arriving on his steamboat from Spain, accompanied by his helpers, the Zwarte Pieten. Between his arrival and December 5, you can find him all across the country, visiting businesses, schools and people's homes, bringing candies, cookies and gifts. He and his helpers may also decide to pay a kid's home a surprise visit at night. In order to limit the excitement, parents usually compromise to having him visit twice a week, say on Tuesday night and Saturday night, in order not to be dragged out of bed at 6 o'clock *every* morning to see if there are any surprises.

Sinterklaas's birthday is not only a holiday for children; grown-ups like to participate in the fun by means of a gift (serious, silly or, often, homemade, called a *surprise*) with an accompanying poem that summarizes the receiver's past year, intermingled with surprising habits and silly mistakes – often in a slightly ridiculing tone. (Bear in mind that the Dutch love to tease and the more fun they make of you, the more they like you, although it has been known to happen that the unsuspecting non-Dutch receiver of such a lovingly and amusingly composed poem has rushed out of the room in tears.)

The phenomenon of Zwarte Piet (Black Pete) tends to surprise visiting foreigners. In this era of post-anti-apartheid and desegregation, what exactly do the Dutch think they're doing with black-face-painted helpers? Well, Sinterklaas's Zwarte Pieten actually represent the Moors of Spain; chased into the Sierra Nevada by the Catholic Spaniards in the 15th century, they apparently sought gainful employment in the services of St. Nicholas. Every now and then, the discussion flares up as to whether Zwarte Piet should be given a different color, or perhaps even completely eliminated – but that is a tough decision. However politically incorrect and insensitive to other races the festivities may seem, there is no indication that the presence of Zwarte Piet at Sinterklaas' side has in any way influenced children's perception of people of another race. In fact, the one that children fear is Sinterklaas – as he is the one who decides whether they are 'good or bad' – while Zwarte Piet is the children's friend and ally.

Zwarte Piet

Christmas

Christmas itself is normally reserved for religious observances and family get-togethers – with some gifts, perhaps, for the kids. The Dutch do not celebrate Christmas Eve – though they do attend church services in the evening – instead they have First and Second Christmas Day. Which lend themselves excellently for visiting first one set of in-laws, and then the next on the next day.

List of Holidays

January 1	New Year's Day
February 14	Valentine's Day
February/March	Carnival
March/April	Good Friday
March/April	*Pasen* – Easter Sunday and Monday

Around Easter, the Dutch eat 32 million eggs

April 27	*Koningsdag* – King's (Birth)day
May 4	*Dodenherdenking* (Commemoration of the Dead)
May 5	*Bevrijdingsdag* (Liberation Day)
May	*Hemelvaartsdag* (Ascension Day)
May, 2nd Sunday	Mother's Day
May/June	*Pinksteren* (Whit Sunday) and *Tweede Pinksterdag* Monday (Whit Monday)
June, 3rd Sunday	Father's Day
September, 3rd Tuesday	*Prinsjesdag* (Opening of Parliament)
October 4	*Dierendag* (International Animal Day)
November 11	St. Maarten
December 5	Sinterklaas
December 25 and 26	First and Second Christmas Day
December 31	New Year's Eve

The Steamier Side of Society

High on the to-do list of every visitor to the Netherlands, right up there with the famed museums, is a walk on the wild side of seemingly sedate Dutch society: a tour of the red-light district in Amsterdam. The *wallen* ('the walls'), as that part of town is known, lives up to its billing. Everything you expect is there. Teeming crowds juxtaposing businessmen and tourists; prostitutes publicly ensconced in the windows of the numerous business establishments; the quote-unquote coffee shops that sell everything from Thai stick to space cakes – coffee definitely not being the specialty of the house.

Every year, more than a million vibrators are sold in the Netherlands

---

Point of View

After soaking in the sights for a few minutes, you may realize that the only thing that makes the goings-on into a spectacle is your point of view. Having spent some time in the Netherlands, you probably aren't surprised that everything is well-organized (the Dutch police even have an English-language how-to guide to help tourists safely explore the steamier side of the city); but you probably did not expect it to be 'dead normal', as the Dutch say. The only difference between the streets of the red-light district and other shopping districts in the city is the merchandise. While there are prostitutes and drugs in every large city, Dutch or otherwise, in the Netherlands both businesses are given an air of legitimacy that exceeds that found in most other countries. Like so many other visitors, you marvel at the tolerant Dutch in action.

Clichés

Noting that the Dutch are tolerant, however, is not exactly a radical discovery. Social experiments in the Netherlands are sufficiently renowned that such comments are almost clichés. But there is more to this than just being open-minded. Most visitors are shocked when they learn that until recently prostitution was illegal and that

'De Wallen' – Red Light District, Amsterdam

the possession or sale of recreational drugs remains against the law. After one day in Amsterdam, it is hard to believe that any of this ever was a criminal offense – which, in a sense, is correct: even when illegal, these activities occurred and thrived with the tacit approval of the local community and the Dutch government.

Tolerance vs. Acceptance

Don't confuse Dutch realism with loose mores. As individuals, most are principled; a fair number are very religious. When asked, the overwhelming majority indicates that they don't use drugs or prostitutes, and the statistics bear this out. Remarkably, the Dutch make a distinction between their values and what they expect from others. While there is general agreement that recreational drugs and prostitution are social evils, there is also a strong consensus that they are going to occur whether they are illegal or not and that prosecution often results in social ails worse than the original malady. Thus, it is better to mitigate the negative aspects of these activities with regulation (what could be more Dutch than that?) than to drive them underground through futile attempts at eradication. That these vices were or are still technically illegal is mostly a reflection of the consensus-building that is implicit to Dutch public policy: it is one thing to passively accept certain activities as inevitable; it is another to actively endorse them. In short, there is a big difference between tolerance and acceptance.

A Work in Progress

Sounds great. But how well do these Dutch approaches work? The answer depends on your priorities. In the case of prostitution, the public-health accomplishments are impressive. Thanks to access to medical care and routine testing, the physical well-being of most prostitutes and their clients is significantly better in the Netherlands than in many other countries. Unfortunately, rules only protect those who are a part of the system, and even then, only those who are able to understand and use them. In particular, many of the prostitutes are thought to be illegal immigrants, including an unknown number who were coerced into the trade and work in de facto slavery. Due to fear of reprisals or deportation, it is less likely that foreign prostitutes will contact the authorities for help if they need it. Recent attempts to expand government control by legalizing brothels may have made things worse: the added expense has driven some activity underground. While such problems are not unique to the Netherlands, the abuse of these individuals, in spite of the existing rules and regulations, is, to say the least, extremely troubling to the Dutch.

Too Pragmatic?

All of this leads some to conclude that the Dutch are too pragmatic. The foreign press invariably carries stories that make you shake your head in wonder, such as the one about the Dutch parents who ran the coffee shop in their town: if their children were going to experiment with controlled substances, they felt better knowing who was selling them the drugs! Nonetheless, in spite of the occasional excesses and the remaining problems, rational social policies as well as systematic and open education on sex, drugs and alcohol have successfully encouraged responsible behavior. As a consequence, most Dutch teenagers choose abstinence or practice safe sex, as evidenced by the low rates of sexually transmitted diseases, teen pregnancies and abortions. (Even dictionaries for Dutch tourists propagate the party line. When it comes to sex, the content is restricted to such useful phrases as 'Only with a condom' and 'Let's not take any chances'). Furthermore, while most Dutch teenagers go through a period of exploration, where some experiment with drugs, most move on: teenage and adult drug usage rates are relatively low.

While it may not be politically or culturally feasible for other countries to adopt these policies or approaches, one cannot help but admire what the Dutch have accomplished.

Alcohol Use and Drugs

Sale of Liquor

From the age of 18 onwards you may legally buy beer, wine and liquor. Alcoholic beverages can be bought in liquor stores and supermarkets – though supermarkets only sell beer, wine and alcoholic beverages with an alcohol percentage up to 12 to 13 percent. Bartenders, liquor dealers and cashiers must ask youngsters who are buying alcohol from them to submit proof of their age, such as a passport, ID-card or driver's license. If any one of these cannot be supplied, they are not allowed to sell it to them.

The Dutch drink an average of 83 liters of beer a year

Drinking and Driving

▶ You may not drive if you are over the 0.5-blood alcohol level or, during the first five years after you have been issued a driver's license; 0.2

▶ This latter limit also applies to drivers of mopeds and motorized bicycles until the age of 24

▶ Driving under the influence is a criminal offense and applies to driving a car and riding a motorcycle, scooter, moped or bicycle

▶ You risk a fine running from 350 euros to 1,600 euros (180 euros to 280 euros, if you are riding a moped or a scooter), depending on your blood alcohol level, plus a possible ban on driving of up to almost a year and possible incarceration

▶ If you are caught driving under the influence of soft or hard drugs, you run the risk of three months of incarceration, having your driver's license suspended for five years, or a fine of up to 7,800 euros.

Drug Use

For the record, trafficking in (importing or exporting), selling, producing and processing either hard or soft drugs are offenses in the Netherlands. The possession of soft drugs (up to 30 grams) or hard drugs (0.5 grams) for personal use is a summary, non-indictable offense. However, as mentioned earlier, if you wish to buy soft drugs, the Netherlands is famous for its coffee shops…

The cheapest and purest cocaine in Europe is sold in the Netherlands and Belgium

Coffee Shops

A coffee shop can best be described as a café that does not sell alcoholic beverages (except in Amsterdam, where some do), but that does sell soft drugs. Low priority is given to the prosecution of coffee shop owners, provided they sell small quantities only and meet the following conditions:

▶ No more than five grams per person are sold in any one transaction
▶ The stock does not exceed 500 grams
▶ No hard drugs are sold
▶ Drugs are not advertised
▶ The coffee shop does not cause any nuisance
▶ No drugs are sold to persons under the age of 18, nor are minors admitted onto the premises.

Per day, the police close an average of 20 illegal cannabis farms. All in all, these plantations, what with enforcement, investigation, stolen electricity and fires, cost the government 447 million euros a year. It is estimated that 60,000 plantations generate an annual turnover of 4 billion euros and legalizing them would fill the state coffers with an additional 850 million euros, if they levied the equivalent of cigarette taxes, as well as 400 million euros if they levied VAT. However, this would not be beneficial for this country's relations with the United Nations, the European Union or the Schengen countries, as the Netherlands has agreed in several treaties that drugs will remain illegal.

Municipalities may set up extra rules, for instance regarding the proximity to schools. Agreements are made with the local police regarding routine checks and the mayor of a city has the authority to close coffee shops that do not meet these conditions.

Coffee shops are not only found in the bigger cities: there are approximately 582 coffee shops, spread over 100-plus municipalities. So don't be surprised if your sleepy little village has one too.

Legal Gymnastics

The Dutch government has to perform legal gymnastics in order to make the sale of soft drugs in coffee shops possible. To make the existence of coffee shops possible, two terms have been introduced: *gedoogbeleid* (policy of tolerance) and *laag opsporingsbeleid* (policy of low investigational priority). The sale of soft drugs in coffee shops is tolerated and, provided the conditions are met, the culturing of soft drugs to be sold via coffee shops will not be prosecuted. The interesting question is: Why is this tolerated? The answer brings to light a specific desire that typifies Dutch society: the aim of this policy is to prevent users of soft drugs from becoming marginalized or being exposed to more harmful drugs.

There are 582 coffee shops in the Netherlands, down from approximately 1,500 20 years ago

Drug Tourism

In an aim to quash drug tourism, if you want to buy drugs, you have to be a legal resident of the Netherlands. It is up to the coffee shop owner to verify this – which, if you think about it, is probably a lot to ask of them…

Though shop owners may not charge VAT over their sales, they do owe income tax over their income; generating a pleasant calculated 400 million euros a year for the state coffers.

Coffeeshop, Amsterdam

Museums

An overview of important, not-to-be missed museums in
the Netherlands in order of top-number of visitors:

**NEMO,
Amsterdam**

**Stedelijk Museum,
Amsterdam**

4

**Anne Frank House,
Amsterdam**

3

**Van Gogh Museum,
Amsterdam**

2

**Rijksmuseum,
Amsterdam**

1

Kröller-Müller
Museum, Otterlo

10

Mauritshuis,
Den Haag

9

Municipal Museum,
The Hague

8

Dutch Open
Air Museum,
Arnhem

7

rmitage,
sterdam

6

1 The Rijksmuseum (English: Imperial Museum) is dedicated
to the arts and history. It is located on the Museum Square in
the borough Amsterdam South, close to the Van Gogh Museum,
the Stedelijk Museum Amsterdam, and the Concertgebouw. The
main building was designed by Pierre Cuypers and first opened
its doors in 1885. On April 13, 2013, after a ten-year renovation
which cost 375 million euros, the main building was reopened by
Queen Beatrix. In that year alone, it attracted 2,220,000 visitors.
It now attracts approximately 3 million visitors a year, making
it the the most visited museum in the Netherlands. On display
are 7,000 objects of art and history, from a total collection of 1
million objects from the years 1200–2000, among which are
masterpieces by Rembrandt, Frans Hals and Johannes Vermeer.

2 The Van Gogh Museum is dedicated to the works of
Vincent van Gogh and his contemporaries and is also located
on the Museum Square. It is located in buildings designed by
Gerrit Rietveld and Kisho Kurokawa. The museum's collection is
the largest collection of Van Gogh's paintings and drawings in the
world. The museum welcomes an annual 1.7 million visitors.

3 **The Anne Frank House** (Dutch: Anne Frank Huis) is a biographical museum dedicated to Jewish wartime diarist Anne Frank. The building is located on a canal called the Prinsengracht, close to the Westerkerk, in central Amsterdam. During World War II, Anne Frank hid from Nazi persecution with her family and four other people in hidden rooms at the rear of this 17th-century canal house, known as the Secret Annex (Dutch: Achterhuis). Anne Frank did not survive the war, but in 1947 her wartime diary was published. In 1957, the Anne Frank Foundation was established to protect the property from developers who wanted to demolish the block. The museum preserves the hiding place, has a permanent exhibition on the life and times of Anne Frank, and has an exhibition space on all forms of persecution and discrimination. The museum attracts an annual 1.2 million visitors and is the 3rd most visited museum in the Netherlands.

4 **The Stedelijk Museum Amsterdam** (Municipal Museum Amsterdam), colloquially known as the Stedelijk, is a museum for modern art, contemporary art, and design, and is located in Amsterdam. The 19th-century building was designed by Adriaan Willem Weissman and the 21st-century wing with the current entrance was designed by Benthem Crouwel Architects. It is located on the Museum Square. The collection comprises modern and contemporary art and design from the early 20th century up to the 21st century. It features artists such as Vincent van Gogh, Wassily Kandinsky, Ernst Ludwig Kirchner, Marc Chagall, Henri Matisse, Jackson Pollock, Karel Appel, Andy Warhol, Willem de Kooning, Marlene Dumas, Lucio Fontana, and Gilbert & George. Annually, the museum welcomes an estimated 675,000 visitors.

5 **Science Museum Nemo** is a science museum in Amsterdam. It is located at the Oosterdok in Amsterdam-Centrum. The museum has its origins in 1923, and, since 1997, is housed in a building designed by Renzo Piano. It contains five floors of hands-on science exhibitions and is the largest science center in the Netherlands. Annually, it attracts almost 600,000 visitors, which makes it the fifth most visited museum in the Netherlands.

6 **The Gemeentemuseum Den Haag** is an art museum in The Hague. The museum, built between 1931 and 1935, was designed by the Dutch architect H.P. Berlage. It is renowned for its large Mondriaan collection, the largest in the world. His last work, *Victory Boogie-Woogie*, is on display here. GEM (museum for contemporary art) and Fotomuseum Den Haag (The Hague museum for photography) are part of the Gemeentemuseum, though not housed in the same building and with a separate entrance fee. The museum's collection of modern art includes works by international artists (Edgar Degas, Claude Monet, Pablo Picasso, Egon Schiele, Frank Stella, Henri Le Fauconnier and many others) and Dutch artists (Charlotte Dumas, Pyke Koch, Piet Mondriaan, Charley Toorop, Jan Toorop, Hans Wilschut and many others). Annually, it attracts almost 600,000 visitors.

7 **The Mauritshuis** (Maurice House) is an art museum in The Hague. The museum houses the Royal Cabinet of Paintings which consists of 841 objects; mostly Dutch Golden Age paintings. The collections contain works by Johannes Vermeer, Rembrandt van Rijn, Jan Steen, Paulus Potter, Frans Hals, Jacob van Ruisdael, Hans Holbein the Younger, and others. Originally, the 17th-century building was the residence of count John Maurice of Nassau. It is now the property of the government of the Netherlands and is listed in the top-100 Dutch heritage sites. Annually, it attracts almost 500,000 visitors.

8 **The Nationaal Militair Museum** (National Military Museum) is situated on the former air base at Soesterberg. It combines the collections of the former Military Aviation Museum in Soesterberg and Army Museum in Delft and its collection runs from arrows from the Stone Age, swords and harnesses from the Middle Ages, to items from the current weapons system of the Dutch army. There are airplanes, canons, and tanks, including seven different jet fighter planes in a 'dogfight', a Leopard 1V and 2 fighter tank, and an M270 Multiple Launch Rocket System (MLRS). A top piece of the collection is the V2, the rocket with which the Germans attacked the Allied Forces in Southern Netherlands, Belgium and England from Northern Netherlands. This was the first operational and steerable rocket. Annually, the museum attracts almost 500,000 visitors.

9 **The Nederlands Openluchtmuseum** (Netherlands Open Air Museum) is an open-air museum and park located near Arnhem with antique houses, farms and factories from different parts of the Netherlands. The Netherlands Open Air Museum focuses on the culture associated with the everyday lives of ordinary people. Annually, it attracts almost 450,000 visitors.

10 **Hermitage Amsterdam** is a branch museum of the Hermitage Museum of Saint Petersburg, Russia, and is located on the banks of the Amstel river in Amsterdam. The museum is located in the former Amstelhof, a classical-style building from 1681. It is currently the largest satellite of the Hermitage and annually attracts more than 400,000 visitors.

Other important museums include Boijmans (Rotterdam), Frans Hals (Haarlem), Kröller-Müller (Otterlo), Bonnefanten (Maastricht) and many, many more. A complete overview can be found on www.artcyclopedia.com/museums/art-museums-in-the-netherlands.html.

GROOT
WOORDENBOEK
VAN DE
NEDERLANDSE
TAAL

GROOT
WOORDENBOEK
VAN DE
NEDERLANDSE
TAAL

GROOT
WOORDENBOEK
VAN DE
NEDERLANDSE
TAAL

a → i

j → r

s → z

van Dale

van Dale

van Dale

The Dutch Language

Learning Dutch

Okay, if you're in one of the bigger cities in Holland, and you venture into the Dutch language, then – at the first trip or hint of an accent – your conversation partner/waiter/storeowner will probably switch to English. Which is probably a relief, but also makes it hard to ever learn the language.

This does not mean, however, that the Dutch are totally okay with your never learning the language – or that you can can get away with English all the time, particularly outside the big cities. The Dutch are very helpful and are proud of their command of the English language, but if, after three or so years, you still cannot order your *volkorenbrood* in Dutch, their font of sympathy might dry up.

Basically, it could be considered a sign of respect to learn the language of your host country, and, if you really want to integrate further, get to know the culture and develop local friendships, you have little choice *but* to learn the language – however daunting it may seem.

The letter E is the most-used letter in the Dutch language

Why Should You Learn Dutch?

If you are the partner or spouse of an employee who has been placed in the Netherlands, you will have time on your hands and find yourself facing the need to navigate daily life in the Dutch language. Wherever you live, you feel more comfortable with your life if you can understand what's going on around you, what it says on the packages in the supermarket, and what that sign means by the bus stop/in the storefront/at the train station.

As for your kids, they will probably pick up the language easily as they play with the kids in the streets, watch Dutch children's TV, or attend school – if they are going to a Dutch one.

How Difficult Is Dutch?

Dutch is not an easy language for English speakers – we simply do not have the capacity for those throaty, guttural sounds on which Netherlandish children are weaned. Sentence structure is awkwardly reversed, and the Dutch love to glue words together into one seemingly endless hangman challenge. Words such as *ziektekostenverzekering* (health care insurance) or *projectontwikkelingsmaatschappijen* (meaning 'property development companies') leave you wondering where one syllable begins and the other ends. If you have some knowledge of German, or perhaps Danish, stored in your brain, you might feel less challenged – but that is only because you've taken this hurdle into a Germanic language before! (Native speakers of these languages, of course, will be at the top of the class.)

The First Steps

You can follow an established course or take private lessons. Holland has a national network of language institutes that offer courses in Dutch to foreigners. These courses are generally referred to as NT2, *Nederlands als tweede taal* (Dutch as a second language). You can find one through your city hall or else by asking around or surfing the Internet. When you have found an institute, they may ask you what type of school you went to at home, what diplomas you have, whether you interact with a lot of Dutch people, whether you have time to go to a school and to do homework, etc. You might also be asked to take a placement exam to determine what level you should pursue. Depending on your specific needs, the institute may suggest an intensive course for quicker immersion.

Dutch numbers require some mental gymnastics – '79' is expressed as 'nine and seventy', for example – so be prepared

A Few Words of Advice

Let the person you're talking to know that you don't (or hardly) speak any Dutch Don't give in to the temptation to do it all in English, as you'll never learn Dutch that way. If you say *Ik wil Nederlands leren*, the Dutch will be more than happy to comply.

Do not be afraid to make mistakes Don't expect to speak Dutch as well as you do your native language – it will only make you insecure, and why demand so much of yourself? Fluency takes much time, and all that matters at first is basic communication.

Pick your moments It isn't always the right moment to insist on speaking Dutch. Be sure there isn't a long line of hurried and harried locals who 'want to get on with their lives' behind you.

Don't make it unnecessarily hard Keep your initial conversations simple.

Don't be afraid to admit you still don't know what they're saying Just say: "Sorry, I'm afraid I still don't get it. Could you repeat it in English, please?" They've just seen you try very hard to connect in their language, and they'll be more than willing to return the effort.

Absorb all day As you hear Dutch in your daily activities, pay attention to what others are saying and how they say it. Look up a word or two at the end of the day, and check out the Dutch subtitles on your favorite TV show. It's a great way to practice.

---

44 million people speak Dutch

Which Dutch?

Not all Dutch people speak the same Dutch language. There is a standard language: *Algemeen Beschaafd Nederlands* (ABN), which translates into the somewhat pompous-sounding 'General Civilized Dutch'. It is what 'well-educated' Dutch people who live in the Randstad (the area comprising Amsterdam, The Hague, Rotterdam, Utrecht and everything in between) speak. This was once the old dialect of the District of Holland, the most powerful province – which is why *Hollands* became the most widespread dialect in the country.

The other regions in the Netherlands speak the same language, but the pronunciation can be quite different and hard to understand at first. Having mastered Dutch in The Hague will not prepare you at all for *Zeeuws*, *Twents*, *Gronings*, *Drents*, or *Brabants* – let alone *Limburgs* (spoken in Limburg), which to many doesn't even *sound* like Dutch, but more like German and Flemish, mixed into one. Also the people from the various cities all have their very distinct way of pronouncing the language. The Dutch can tell within a sentence whether someone is from The Hague, Amsterdam, Rotterdam or Utrecht.

In Friesland, a province in the northwest of Holland, aside from Dutch, they speak Frisian. Many of the words used are the same – but pronounced differently – but they also have a whole unique vocabulary. An interesting factoid to note is that Frisian is considered, historically, to be closer to the English language than Dutch is.

The End Result

If you are planning on staying here for a long time, learning Dutch will help you integrate. In fact, in our item on *Inburgering – Integrating into Dutch Society*, you will read that in many cases, you are obligated to learn the language if you plan on building a life here. How far you get will depend on whether or not you have the time, talent and inclination to master another language. If you decide to go for it, we wish you luck and fun! And don't forget, just about any foreign accent will give the Dutch language something extra to make it a little more palatable.

Website

▶ www.netinnederland.nl: an online platform to help newcomers to the Netherlands learn Dutch and become familiar with Dutch society through watching some of the most popular television programs which have been given subtitles in English.

Dutch Words that Made It into English

- *Baas* turned into *boss*. The true origin of the word is a bit blurry but a Dutch ship's captain was called 'baas' in the 17th century.
- *Vrolijk* (cheerful, jolly) found its way into English as *frolic*, a romp.
- *Grof* (coarse) turned into *gruff* in English. Is this another character trait attributed to the Dutch? It is called 'direct' in today's speech.
- *Kielhalen* became *keelhauling,* probably because the Dutch liked to do a lot of it. It's one of many nautical terms the seafaring Dutch contributed to the English language. *Sloep (sloop), jacht (yacht), schoener (schooner)* and, inevitably, *wrak (wreck)* are some of them.
- *Kwakzalver* was shortened to *quack*. Have a look at Jan Steen's version of one in the Rijksmuseum. His paintings provide an interesting peek into the lives of ordinary people in the 17th century.
- *Koekje* became *cookie*.
- *Dijk* turned into *dike*. The Dutch never stopped talking about dikes and the word seeped into the English language through sheer force of usage.
- *Accijns* turned into *excise* by way of *excijs*, or *tax*. A Dutch invention if ever there was one.
- *Droge waere*. A middle Dutch phrase meaning '*dry wares'*. This may be the origin of '*drugs'*.
- *Polder*, *pomp* became *polder* and *pump*, another obvious reference to the Dutch obsession with getting that darned water out and keeping it out.
- *Apartheid*. Separateness. Obviously not a word to be proud of, referring to the separation in society of races.
- *Santa Claus*. The name Santa Clause originated from the other Dutch name for Saint Nicholas; *Sinterklaas*.

- *Yankee*. One of the theories of the origin of this word is that it is based on the 'common' Dutch name Jan Kees.
- *Kool sla*, or cabbage salad, became *cole slaw*.
- *De kooi*, or the cage used to capture wildfowl, became *decoy*.
- *Ontlopen*, to run away or avoid, became *elope*.
- The *ezel*, used by Dutch painters (and which also means donkey), became the *easel*.
- The *rugzak*, a bag we carry on our backs, became a *rucksack*.

A good book on the subject is: *Cookies, Coleslaw, and Stoops: The Influence of Dutch on the North American Languages*, by Nicoline van der Sijs

Essential Dutch Expressions

You may be learning Dutch, you may be ignoring the language altogether or you may be a fluent speaker. Here is a handy list of 10 Dutch expressions which everyone needs to know.

- *Doe maar normaal dan doe je al gek genoeg*. Just behave normally; this is already crazy enough. Guess the translation says all.
- *Heb ik wat van je aan?* When you look at a Dutch person fixedly they may ask you if they are wearing something of yours. This is not meant kindly so take care not to stare.
- *Daarom* (pronounced: *derooom*). This means 'exactly' and is an expression of concurrence. However, it usually has nothing to do with what the other speaker has just said. It's either an excuse to take over the conversation or a ploy to mask the fact that you have been fast asleep for the last five minutes.
- *Krijg toch de tering/kanker/typhus*. "Get TB/cancer/typhoid" – take your pick – is an example of the Dutch predilection for wishing nasty diseases on people. Sometimes followed by *achter je hart* (behind your heart).

- *Ik zeg maar zo, ik zeg maar niks.* I'll just say I say nothing. Typical example of Dutch poldering: prudent, non-committal, on the fence.
- *Dat kan niet.* It can't be done, impossible. Phrase familiar to expats faced with Dutch bureaucracy.
- *Doe effe normaal.* Behave. Made famous by Geert Wilders who said it to the prime minister in parliament, this expression is indicative of the Dutch wish to appear 'normal' and not stand out.
- *Doe je dat (bij je moeder) thuis ook?* Do you do that at home too? Used by suicidal train staff when they see three thugs with their feet on the opposite seats.
- *Op één been kun je niet lopen.* You can't walk on one leg. An excuse for having another one.
- *Kinderen die vragen worden overgeslagen.* Children who ask won't get anything. A good Calvinistic tradition that has fallen into disuse.
- *Hoge bomen vangen veel wind.* High trees catch a lot of wind. People who distinguish themselves often attract criticism.
- *Ben je in de kerk geboren?* Were you born in a church? Used when somebody doesn't shut the door when leaving a room.
- *Die is niet goed in z'n bovenkamer.* He is not well in his upstairs room. Meaning he is nuts.
- *Hij ziet ze vliegen.* He can see them flying. Meaning he is nuts.

Living in the Netherlands

Your First Steps

Arrivals 1-2
Aankomst

Departures 1-2
Vertrek

Check-in 1-16

Visa, MVV and Residence Permit

Visa

Depending on your nationality, you will have to request a visa, (called Visum Kort Verblijf [VKV], or Short Stay Visa) before entering the country if you want to come here for a period shorter than 90 days. Which countries these are, and how you go about arranging the visa, you will find on the website listed below.

MVV (Authorization Temporary Stay)

If you want to come to the Netherlands for a period exceeding 90 days, you must arrange an authorization temporary stay (MVV). To do this, you visit the Netherlands embassy in your country of origin or residence and initiate the so-called TEV procedure, whereby you apply for both an MVV and a residence permit at the same time. If you have a sponsor (a person or organization with an interest in your coming to the Netherlands, such as a family member, employer or university) in the Netherlands, your sponsor can start the TEV procedure, by filling in the application form, including the requested documents, and sending this to the IND.

You must await the decision on the TEV procedure abroad. Only under exceptional circumstances can you travel to the Netherlands before being issued the MVV: however, before doing this, you must report these circumstances to the IND.

If the IND decides that there is no objection to your entry in the Netherlands, it sends an MVV-approval to the Dutch embassy in your home country/ country of legal residence and also issues your residence permit so that you need not apply for it separately.

Before traveling to the Netherlands, you collect the authorization temporary stay at the Dutch Embassy or Consulate in your home country/country of legal residence. Once you have arrived in the Netherlands you collect your residence document in person within two weeks at the IND desk. Note: You cannot apply for a residence permit if you entered the Netherlands without making use of the MVV.

In order to be able to issue you your residence document, the IND needs your fingerprints, passport photo and signature. Please check with the IND as to how and where you can provide these. An MVV must also be requested for your accompanying family members. Processing time is approximately 90 days.

MVV Not Required
The following persons do not need an MVV:

▶ EU/EEA and Swiss Nationals: If you are a national of any of the European Union (EU) or European Economic Area (EEA) member states or Switzerland, you will not need an authorization temporary stay prior to traveling to the Netherlands. Formally, EU/EEA and Swiss nationals also do not need a residence permit; however, if you intend to stay here longer than four months, you will have to register with the municipality.
▶ Some Non EU/EEA/Swiss Nationals: You are exempted from the need to arrange an authorization temporary stay if you are from the United States, Canada, Japan, South Korea, Monaco, Vatican City, Australia or New Zealand.

Residence Permit (VVR-Procedure)
If you are exempted from the need to arrange an MVV, you can apply for a residence permit with the IND. Or your prospective employer can apply for the residence permit while you are still living abroad.

Required Documents
The documents that you have to submit when registering and/or applying for a residence permit are, among others:

▶ A legalized certified copy of your birth certificate (also your spouse's or partner's)
▶ A legalized marriage license, if applicable

▶ If either you or your partner were previously married, a copy of the legalized divorce decree

▶ Whatever else you need depends on your circumstances and country of origin. Other documents, such as a passport, work permit and proof of insurance will be required at some later point, check with the IND what these are.

Registering with the Municipality

If you are planning on staying in the Netherlands longer than four months, you have to report with the municipality (*stadhuis* or *gemeentehuis*) to have yourself entered in the municipal register (*bevolkingsregister*). In order to be able to do this, you must first arrange 'suitable housing', which you demonstrate by means of a rental contract, purchase contract or a statement drawn up by the person in whose house you will officially be living.

Non-residents staying in the Netherlands for a period not exceeding four months also have to register, but as non-residents (RNI).

Your Stay Exceeds Five Years

If you have legally resided in the Netherlands for a period of five years, you qualify for the residence document 'long-term residence of citizens of the Union'. You are, however, not *obligated* to request this.

Websites

▶ Visa requirements: www.government.nl

▶ MVV requirements: https://ind.nl/en

▶ Health insurance: www.government.nl/topics/health-insurance

DigiD

In order to file your online tax return, check out what your health insurance has paid for you, arrange benefits, order online municipal documents, etc., you need your digital identity, known as your DigiD. If you don't do any of this online, you can do without it – but what are the chances of that?

To arrange a DigiD, you have to register with the municipality in which you live, and make sure you have a *burgerservicenummer* (BSN). Then you visit www.digid.nl, where you fill in your *burgerservicenummer*, date of birth, postal code, and house number. Here you also choose a username and a password. Five days after you do this, you will receive your activation code by mail, which you must use within 20 days, together with your username and password, to activate your personal DigiD.

The most common surname in the US is Smith; in the world, Chang; and in the Netherlands, De Jong

---

Citizen Service Number

Everyone who registers with a municipality in the Netherlands is issued a Citizen Service Number (*burgerservicenummer*, BSN) within a few days. Without this, your employer will not be able to withhold your social security contributions. Here, employers withhold these contributions and pay them to the tax authorities for you. You also need it to arrange your health care insurance and register with temp agencies. Also expat family members have to obtain a Citizen Service Number.

If you are not a resident of the Netherlands or will be staying here fewer than four months, but need to deal with Dutch government institutions – for instance, because you are working here temporarily, or live abroad but receive a Dutch pension – you need to register with the Basisregistratie Personen (Basic Registration), which registers both residents and non-residents. You will be registered with the Registratie Niet-Ingezetenen (RNI, Registration of Non-Residents) and issued a *burgerservicenummer*. This you can use to arrange tax-related matters, but also benefits, such as the General Old Age Pension (AOW), if you live abroad.

Refugees

Seeking Asylum
If you have come to the Netherlands to seek asylum, you report with the reception center of the IND. After this has been done, the COA (Central Organization for the Reception of Asylum Seekers) receives you in their central location in Ter Apel (Groningen), where the Aliens Police registers you and verifies your identity, and the Health Services test you for TBC. You spend a maximum of four days there, after which you are taken to a home for refugees. During this time VluchtelingenWerk Nederland (Dutch Council for Refugees) and the Raad van Rechtsbijstand (Legal Aid Council) assist you with the preparation of your request.

In the infographic on page 120-121 you will find more information on the subsequent process.

Working
If you have applied for asylum, you may not work during the first 6 months of your asylum procedure. After that you are allowed to work for 24 of every 52 weeks, while the application is still being processed. You will need a work permit (TWV, issued by the UWV), which your employer applies for. You can work up to 40 hours a week, but you cannot earn more than 14 euros a hour, which will be deducted from your benefit.

Studying
Those who have refugee status or are asylum seekers and are starting a higher education can approach Stichting UAF Steunpunt

(www.uaf.nl) for more information on the possibilities of a grant. On their website, click on the little British flag on the left-hand side of the screen to access more information.

Types of Refugees

There is a considerable difference between refugees who reside in emergency shelters and those who live in refugee centers. When you first enter the country, you are housed in emergency shelters, such as a sports center, a tented camp, an old school or a converted homeless shelter. All you have is a roof over your head and three meals a day. If you live in a refugee center, and have already entered the official procedure, you have a right to more amenities, such as:

A certain amount of money a week, depending on whether or not you are here alone, or as part of a family, as well as the meal arrangements. You will receive (approximately):

Responsible for your own meals:

No. of people	amount received p.p.	amount received per child (<18 yrs) p.w.
1–2	45 euros	35 euros
3	37 euros	29 euros
4 or more	33 euros	26 euros

Dinners is served every day:

No. of people	amount received p.p.	amount received per child (<18 yrs) p.w.
1–2	28 euros	19 euros
3	23 euros	16 euros
4 or more	21 euros	14 euros

You will also receive a weekly allowance of 13 euros a week, to spend on, for instance, clothes or toys. The COA arranges a bank account for you on which it deposits this money. If you have money of your own somehow, you will receive less from the government. If you have a home, you will receive a loan with which to pay for things such as a bed, a couch, a table and a refrigerator.

Education

As all children have a so-called 'education obligation', also refugee children will have to go to school. Every refugee center is linked to an elementary school, but the children are not obligated to attend this particular school.

First they go to an international class, until their Dutch is good enough for them to attend the regular classes. If you are not of school age, you are given lessons in the Dutch language, as well as additional courses, and receive help in looking for a job.

Health Care

Every refugee has pretty much the same health insurance as Dutch citizens who take out the basic insurance. This means that visits to the GP, antibiotics and maternity care (assistance after giving birth) are covered. However, if you want to stop smoking, this is not covered...

Day
3+4

Day
1+2

Registration
and reception

Arrival
NL

Residence permit

Acceptation

Extended procedure

Rejection

Appeal

Return

Visiting a specialist becomes a little more complicated. Together with an insurance company, the COA has assigned a number of specialists to take care of refugees. However, to visit them, you must first request permission so that they can ensure you need to see one. (This is not really any different for Dutch citizens; they also need to see their GP first before being referred to a specialist).

Duties

As a refugee, you will have to report with the Aliens Police and the COA on a regular basis. You have to register with your municipality within six months. And all refugee centers have rules that you will have to respect.

Websites

▶ COA: www.coa.nl/en
▶ Studying for refugees: www.uaf.nl/home/english
▶ www.vluchtelingenwerk.nl/english
▶ www.netinnederland.nl: this online platform was launched to help newcomers to the Netherlands learn Dutch and become familiar with Dutch society through watching some of the most popular television programs which have been given subtitles in English, Arabic and Dutch
▶ DigiD: www.digid.nl/english

Inburgering – Integrating into Dutch Society

On the official Dutch government website – www.rijksoverheid.nl – it is stated that the government is of the opinion that it is important that anyone living in the Netherlands participate in Dutch society. For instance, by working here or studying here. And that one condition for being able to do this is to learn the language.

In fact, it states that if you are not from an EU/EEA country, Switzerland or Turkey and are coming here for a longer period of time, you are *obligated* to learn the Dutch language as part of the obligated *inburgeringscursus*, which has been translated into everything from the mild-sounding 'newcomers' course' to the more off-putting sounding 'civic integration exam'. In any case, the idea is for you to learn the language, get to know Dutch society and find a way to become economically independent as quickly as possible.

Of course, if you come here as a foreign student and follow one of the more than 2,000 English-language courses, then you can probably get by just fine 'participating in Dutch society as a student' without learning a whole lot of Dutch. The same goes, if you come here to work for an international company where little, if any, knowledge of the Dutch language is required of you. Furthermore, as everyone in the stores, bars and restaurants will switch to English anyway once they detect an accent or a struggle with the language, there will probably be no actual stimulus to learn the language. Which is why it has been stated that anyone who comes here temporarily – such as a student or an expat – does not have to take the course.

The 'exam' has therefore been created for everyone who wants to come here and build up a life. Before actually moving here, depending on your nationality, you must take an exam (the Basic Civic Integration Examination Abroad) at the Dutch consulate or embassy in your country of residence – or a neighboring country if your country does not have one – in order to be issued a provisional residence permit (MVV) with which you can legally enter the country. To do this, you register via the site www.naarnederland.nl (to the Netherlands), after which you can download an 'official self-study pack' with which to prepare for the three parts of the exam: Knowledge of Dutch Society, Speaking and Reading. Most questions are multiple choice and if you have passed one part of the exam, you do not have to redo it when you retake the parts you did not pass. Once you have passed this exam in its entirety, you are issued the MVV with which you can legally enter the country, register with the municipality you will be living in, and request a residence permit.

Once in the Netherlands, you take the second portion of the exam, which focuses on additional issues such as how to find a job, how to make an appointment at the hospital, and what types of schools there are (for if you have children). You have three years to pass the exam – if you don't, you receive a fine and you 'might be' refused a permanent residence permit. Refugees are not denied a permanent residence permit on these grounds.

Alternatives to taking this exam are obtaining your diploma Dutch as a Second Language (Nederlands als Tweede Taal) of following a vocational training. For other exceptions and additional rules, you can check out any of the two websites listed here.

Dutch society is known as a 'caring society'; it helps drug addicts reintegrate into society, it protects prostitutes against disease and abuse, it is in the top-5 of countries that give the most to charity, and it pays out a lot of benefits to help those who (temporarily) cannot help themselves. In keeping with this mindset is the brochure for those whose partner wants to come live in the Netherlands too, in which you will find words to the wise such as: "Once in the Netherlands, they will have to get used to their new circumstances. You can imagine that homesickness, loneliness and a lack of social contacts could be among the problems your partner is faced with. There is always somewhere you can turn to with your or your partner's problems." And they go on to list a few. But that is not all; once your partner is here, and preparing for the exam, the brochure urges you to: "Practice with your partner, speak as much Dutch as possible with each other and … explain the Netherlands and its customs to him or her." How many government institutions do you know that will take the trouble to place themselves in their immigrants' partner's shoes, so that they can advise the immigrant on how to help their partner integrate into society? And then sit down and write the text, have a meeting to agree that yes, this is how they want to put it, and then publish it? It is really quite endearing.

Websites
▶ www.inburgeren.nl
▶ www.duo.nl
▶ www.netinnederland.nl

Obligation to Carry ID

Everyone over the age of 13 must carry some form of legal ID at all times; this being a passport (for EU nationals) or a valid aliens document (for non-EU nationals). Dutch nationals may show either a driver's license, a passport, or an identity card. Photocopies are not allowed, nor is inviting the police officer to your home to check your documents. Children over the age of 13 must have their own papers; inclusion in their parents' passport is not enough.

Who is authorized to ask you to show your papers? The police are, as well as parking inspectors, officers of the Health and Safety Inspectorate, inspectors from the Building Control Department, tax inspectors, customs inspectors, forest rangers (whom you will meet while walking your dog), school inspectors, etc. And, of course, but this is a totally different type of situation, you show your ID when opening a bank account, requesting a government benefit, starting a new job, etc. – AND when attending a soccer game…

The purpose of this obligation is to help combat crime and you may only be requested to show your documents if there is a valid reason – for instance, if you have committed a (traffic) offense or crime, are using public transportation without having paid for it, or if the police needs your assistance, for instance to help solve a crime, or to maintain the public order. The request must be in keeping with the position of the person asking you for your ID. In other words, a tax inspector cannot detain you for this purpose in connection with running a red light.

If you refuse to comply, you may be taken to the police station for identification and run the risk of owing a 2,250-euro fine (in extreme cases – in most cases, the fine will be more reasonable; more in the vicinity of 45 euros, for those younger than 16, and 90 euros for those older than 16).

Store and building security officers may ask you for your ID, but you do not have to show it. However, they are then allowed to deny you entry or to escort you out of the building.

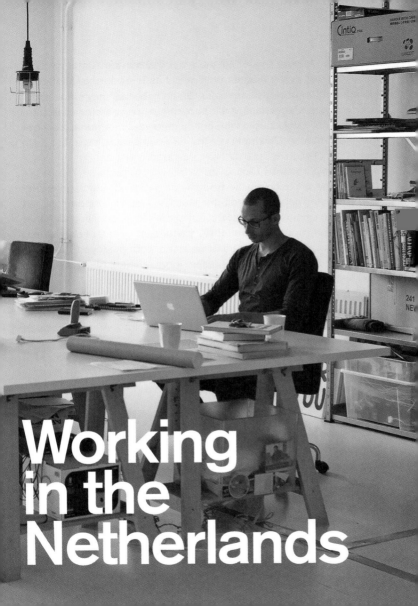

Working
in the
Netherlands

A Job

In terms of number of jobs, the commercial service sector remains the strongest in the Netherlands, and has been for several years, closely followed by the health care and manufacturing industries. Also science & engineering are showing growth as they search for international and capable workers in areas such as water management, green and renewable energy, as well as logistics.

Dutch Employment Law

Unless you are working here under an expat contract governed by your home country laws, the Dutch rules on employment will apply to you. Even expatriates, whose contract explicitly states that a foreign law applies to the employment relationship, will find that they are subject to mandatory rules of Dutch employment, thanks to international private law. Let's take a look at a few topics.

Probation Period

Type of Contract	Maximum Duration of Probation
Contract for less than 6 months	no probation period
Contract between 6 months and 2 years	1 month
2-year or permanent contract	2 months

The Netherlands has the highest percentage of part-time employees in the EU

Chain Contracts

Chain contracts sounds rather vague, but what the term refers to is a chain of employment contracts for a limited period of time. In order to protect employees against employers who try to avoid offering them a permanent employment contract by means of a series of temporary ones, it has been decided after three consecutive fixed-period contracts – or if the fixed-term contracts exceed two years in total – the employment contract is deemed to be a contract for an indefinite period of time, even if it is explicitly stated that it is a fixed-term contract. Only if a period of more than six months has passed between contracts is this fictional 'chain' broken and does the counting start from the beginning. These rules do not apply to certain types of work, nor to employees who are younger than 18 years of age.

Min/Max/Zero Hours

If you work on call, there are two types of contracts you can enter into. One is the min/max contract:: this offers you a guaranteed number of hours of work (and pay) as well as the possibility that your employer will call you in to work more hours. Every time you are called in, you receive a minimum of three hours' pay. A maximum number of hours can also be set per time you are called in. It offers you certain rights that all employees have, such as continued pay (70 percent) during illness, protection against dismissal, and the accrual of holiday allowance, as well as the obligation on your side to show up if you are called in. After the first six months have passed, you receive wages based on your average number of hours worked over the past three months.

There is also the 'nul-uren contract' (zero hours contract), which does not offer a minimum number of hours, but does require your employer to pay you at least three hours every time he calls you in. It offers you the same rights and obligations as the min/max contract.

Dismissal

If something has happened that has damaged your work relationship, your employer has to terminate the employment contract via the sub-district sector of the District Court (or Cantonal Court). If the reason for dismissal is long-term illness on your side, the employment contract can be terminated via the UWV (Employee Insurance Agency). Other ways to terminate an employment agreement are: by mutual consent, during the probationary period, or through summary dismissal for 'urgent cause'.

For employees who have been employed for a minimum of two years, a so-called transition compensation is due. See below.

Notice Period

When terminating the employment contract, your employer must apply the following notice periods (unless the employment contract is dissolved by the courts, or unless the end date is linked to a specific project or temporary replacement of another employee):

Length of employment period	Notice period
0 – 5 years	1 calendar month
5 – 10 years	2 calendar months
10 – 15 years	3 calendar months
> 15 years	4 calendar months

If you have a temporary employment contract of longer than six months, your employer must notify you one month in advance. For temp contracts with a duration of less than six months, termination can be with immediate effect.

For you, the employee, the notice period is always one month. You can agree differently, in which case the agreed-upon notice period for the employee is doubled for the employer. Collective labor agreements (CAOs) can provide for different (and even equal) notice periods.

Severance Payment/Transition Payment

Severance payment can be granted either as a lump sum (known as a 'golden handshake'), or as a periodically paid supplement to the unemployment benefit or lower wages in the next job. This so-called transition payment (*transitievergoeding*) is calculated as follows: 1/3 of your monthly salary for every year of employment if you were employed for a period shorter than 10 years. If you were employed longer than 10 years, you receive 1/3 of your monthly salary per year related to the first ten years and 1/2 of your monthly salary per year related to the years in excess of 10 years.

Employment Agency

Employment agencies are expected to treat you equally to employees who are in the employment of the company to which you are sent to work when it comes to wages, working on holidays, night shifts, overtime, vacation days, compensation, etc.

The collective labor agreement (CAO) of the ABU (Federation of Private Employment) applies to foreign temps, also those who have been recruited to work in the Netherlands via an agency. You can find the details of this CAO on the ABU website, in English, Polish, German, Arabic and Turkish. The site is listed below. It applies to all employment agencies, thus also to (foreign) employment agencies that place employees on the Dutch labor market from abroad. Furthermore, nationals of the European Economic Area (EEA) can move to the Netherlands for work and enjoy the same conditions as Dutch nationals in areas such as access to housing, wages and social security – among others.

Language

Unless you have been sent here by a company and will remain working in an English-language (or any other foreign language environment), you probably won't be able to get by without learning Dutch. In fact, the government has determined that if you work in a 'risky' work environment (manning large machines, or removing asbestos, for instance), you have to be able to speak Dutch, in order to be able to function safely and avoid accidents. The level of your job and responsibilities will determine the level of Dutch required.

The ability to speak English fluently, however, will often come in handy in this internationally-oriented economy. But don't forget, the Dutch speak the language quite well, so it won't be enough to land you the job!

For more on language courses, see our pages on *Learning Dutch*.

Don't forget to check out the rules on work permits, in our item Work Permits, and the need for a BSN (*burgerservicenummer*)

Websites

- ▶ Collective Labor Agreement Foreign Temp Agencies: www.abu.nl
- ▶ UWV: www.uwv.nl
- ▶ Finding a job:
  - www.linkedin.com
  - www.monsterboard.nl
  - www.intermediair.nl
  - www.stepstone.nl
  - www.iamexpat.nl/career/jobs-netherlands
  - www.expatica.com
  - www.englishlanguagejobs.com
  - www.togetherabroad.nl
  - www.oneworld.nl
  - www.jobbird.com
  - www.nationalevacaturebank.nl
  - www.fd.nl

Work Permit

EU/EEA/Switzerland

If you want to work in the Netherlands, you will need a work permit, unless you are a citizen of an EU/EEA country, Switzerland or Japan. Though Croatia joined the EU in 2013, Croatian citizens still need a work permit – at least until 2018.

Single Permit

If you are a national of any other country and want to work here longer than three months, you will have to request a GVVA (Gecombineerde Vergunning voor Verblijf en Arbeid, Combined Permit for Living and Working), which you request from the Immigration and Naturalization Services (IND). This also applies if you come here to gain work experience as a trainee or apprentice.

Work Permit

You do not need a GVVA, but do have to request a work permit from the UWV (Dutch Employee Insurance Agency) if you:

- ► Are staying here shorter than three months
- ► Have come here to do seasonal labor
- ► Are a student
- ► Are a refugee
- ► Have been sent here by an international group of companies
- ► Are Croatian.

Further Conditions

If you are not from an EEA-country, you can only work here if your employer cannot find someone suitable to do the job within the EEA, the job has been on the market for at least five weeks (or, as the case may be; three months), and your employer can show he has done his utmost to find someone on the EEA market.

Further Exceptions

You also don't have to arrange a work permit if:

- ► You come here as Knowledge Migrant
- ► Your residence permit states that you are free to work here
- ► You are self-employed and are doing work that is listed on your residence permit
- ► You in principle require a work permit, but are working here in the employment of a service provider to whom the free movement of employment applies (for instance, another European country).

Students

As a non-Dutch (PhD) graduate or scientific researcher, you can stay/come here to look for a job after graduation. The following conditions apply:

Graduated here	Graduated abroad
Time to look for a job: 1 year	Time to look for a job: 1 year
Upon graduation, you have three years to stay here and look for a job	Upon graduation, you have three years to come here and look for a job
No work permit required	No work permit required
Also applies if you have a Bachelor's Degree	Does not apply if you have a Bachelor's Degree
Must show a certified copy of the diploma	Must have the diploma valuated by EP-Nuffic
You must be able to support yourself during this search – else you could forfeit your permit	You must be able to support yourself during this search – else you could forfeit your permit

Once you have found a job, your employer must initiate the GV-VA-procedure, requesting both a work permit and a residence permit. If you meet the requirements for being a Knowledge Migrant, you request a residence permit for Knowledge Migrants. If you start your own company, and meet the conditions, you change your residence permit to one for self-employed persons. If you are an EU/EEA or Swiss national, you are free to work here (an exception applies to Croatians).

Highly Skilled Migrants

In order to improve the position of the Netherlands as a knowledge economy and to make it more attractive as a work location for highly skilled migrants from outside the EU/EEA, it has created a policy aimed at simplifying their entry into the country. To enter the country as a highly skilled migrant, you need either an MVV and a residence permit or, if you do not need an MVV, merely a residence permit. You do not need a work permit. Only a recognized sponsor, your employer, can submit a request for this with the IND.

Also guest lecturers, scientific researchers and medical trainees are regarded as highly skilled migrants.

European Blue Card
The European Blue Card has been created for non-EU employees who come to carry out highly qualified work in the EU. The conditions are stricter than those for Highly Skilled Migrants. You can find these on the website listed below.

The Blue Card not only allows you to work in the Netherlands without the need for a work permit, but after 18 months you and your family can live and work elsewhere in the EU as well.

Spiritual Counsellors or Ministers of Religion
Special rules apply to these persons. They can be found on the IND website.

Family Members
If you have a partner or relative who has permission to live and work in the Netherlands, you may be able to obtain a residence permit for the purpose of family reunification, which would give you the same rights as your family member. If they have permission to work, you *may* be exempt from the need for a separate work permit.

Please note! If a family member who is not an EU/EEA or Swiss citizen intends to stay with you in the Netherlands, you have to register with the IND.

A Few Other Rules
▶ If you **change employers**, the new employer must also have a work permit in your name.
▶ The single permit is issued for up to three years.
▶ A work permit is **valid** for the duration of your employment contract, up to a maximum of five years, but can be extended.
▶ **Students** can work while studying, but there are restrictions for non-EU/EEA/Swiss/Japanese nationals: you can only work up to 10 hours per week, or full-time for seasonal work in June,

July and August. In both cases, your employers will need a work permit in your name.

▶ If you don't need a work/single permit, you can work as soon as you have your residence permit, which you can collect upon arrival in the Netherlands.

▶ To carry out research at a recognized **research** institute, your institute applies for a residence permit for scientific research on your behalf. You do not need a work permit to carry out the research work, but if you take on any other type of work in addition, then the employer will need to obtain a work permit in your name.

▶ To work here as an **au pair**, you must go though an au pair agency approved by the Dutch immigration authorities. The agency will arrange a year-long residence permit for you, including permission to work (for more information, see website listed below).

▶ If you want to work here in **self-employment**, you will need an MVV or a residence permit (for more information, see website listed below).

Websites
▶ Conditions Highly Skilled Migrants: ind.nl/EN/individuals/residence-wizard/work/highly-skilled-migrant
▶ Conditions European Blue Card: ind.nl/EN/individuals/residence-wizard/work/EUbluecard/
▶ Au pairs: ind.nl/EN/business/au-pair-agency/au-pair
▶ Self-employment: ind.nl/EN/individuals/residence-wizard/work/working-on-a-self-employed-basis
▶ EP-Nuffic: www.ep-nuffic.nl

Starting Your Own Company

If you are orienting yourself on becoming an entrepreneur, or at least self-employed, these pages offer you some helpful tips.

Chambers of Commerce

The Chambers of Commerce (Kamers van Koophandel) register (practically) all companies based in Holland, whether they are of Dutch or foreign origin. Private persons who work on a free-lance basis and persons who carry out one of the professions specified on the professions list of the Chamber of Commerce, are also obligated to register.

The Chamber of Commerce has an information desk that can provide you with information on how to start a business, which diplomas you need for your specific line of business, how to write a business plan to be able to finance your ideas and what (zoning) plans your municipality has within the area in which you want to establish your firm.

MKB-Nederland

MKB-Nederland (Instituut voor Midden- en Kleinbedrijf) represents the interests of small and medium-sized companies. Various activities are initiated by this institute, aimed at offering its members relevant knowledge and expertise as well as at improving the general position of small and medium-sized companies.

Both banks and the national tax office have information desks for people who plan to start their own business and can provide you with the information you need. The banks might be able to offer you financial assistance as well. All major cities have a business desk at the town hall. An excellent step-by-step guide in English can be found on: www.answersforbusiness.nl/guide/starting-business.

Proof of Identity

When registering with the Chamber of Commerce, you need to

bring valid proof of identity (such as a passport, residence permit or driver's license) together with an original bank statement on your name or an original extract from the population register (not older than one month).

Setting Up Establishment

There are no specific restrictions for foreign companies who wish to start a business in the Netherlands, nor are there restrictions on the ownership of real estate or on the remission of capital and profits abroad.

There are various legal entities that you can set up:

- ► Branch office
- ► *Eenmanszaak*: a one-man business
- ► *Maatschap*: partnership – business involving more than one person, usually used by accountants, doctors, etc.
- ► *Vennootschap onder firma* (VOF): general or commercial partnership – business involving more than one person, under a common name, each severally liable
- ► *Commanditaire vennootschap* (CV): limited partnership with managing and 'silent' partners
- ► *Besloten vennootschap* (BV): private company with limited liability
- ► *Naamloze vennootschap* (NV): (public) corporation.

Taxes self-employed persons
If you run your own business you can be held liable for the following:

- ► Wage tax
- ► Income tax
- ► National insurance schemes
- ► Employee insurance schemes
- ► VAT (value added tax).

If you run a one-man business, you owe income tax and VAT.

Health Care Insurance

You must arrange your own medical insurance, for which you owe a fixed contribution and an income-dependent contribution. If your income lies below a certain level, you can apply for government assistance in paying for this insurance, called the *zorgtoeslag*.

VAT

If you deliver services and goods in the Netherlands, you are obligated to charge your customers VAT (*Belasting Toegevoegde Waarde* or BTW), which you subsequently pay to the tax authorities. The general VAT rates are 21 percent and 6 percent. You owe this, no matter whether you (aim to) make a profit or not, the moment an invoice is sent out. To the delivery of goods and services outside the Netherlands, other rules apply.

The amount of VAT that you have paid to others who deliver their goods and services to you, can be deducted from the amount of VAT you owe. If your 'VAT income' does not exceed a certain amount, you enjoy a full or limited exemption from paying the amount due to the tax authorities.

The amount of VAT due should be reported on the *Aangifte omzetbelasting*, or Turnover Tax Return, on a regular basis (monthly, quarterly or yearly). This is done online, by means of the so-called electronic, or *electronische*, Tax Return. The tax authorities issue you a username and a password to do this.

VAR

Until recently, in order to avoid unpleasant (tax) surprises – for you and your client – you requested the tax authorities to issue you a *Verklaring Arbeidsrelatie* (Statement on Your Labor Relation). This VAR either stated that you were not working in the employment of your client, but for yourself, or that you were working on the basis of a (fictitious) labor relationship. This way, your clients knew upfront whether or not they would have to withhold wage tax or social security contributions on what they paid out to you.

This statement is to be replaced by standard contracts, made up by the tax authorities, which can be downloaded from their site. You are not obligated to make use of such a contract – it just offers you and your clients more clarity.

Tax Deductions

There are a variety of tax deductions, which you can find on the site of the tax authorities. These include a deduction for self-employed persons, a starting entrepreneurs' deduction, a starting disabled entrepreneur's deduction, among others.

Diplomas/Permits

Depending on the type of business you want to start, there are a number of diplomas you might need. For most types of businesses, however, no diploma is required. Keep in mind that some businesses are subject to a zoning plan, or require a building permit, environmental permit or establishment permit. Before you start your business, contact your municipality or the Chamber of Commerce to find out which permits and/or diplomas you may need.

If you have obtained a diploma in another country, this diploma can be evaluated by IDW (www.idw.nl), to see whether it qualifies.

Free-Lancing

There are two ways you can go about free-lancing; either as a self-employed person or through an employment agency. In the first case, you can read about some of the rules that apply to you in these paragraphs; in the latter case, you are, in principle, treated as an employee of the employment agency for tax purposes.

Websites
▶ www.answersforbusiness.nl/guide/starting-business
▶ Dutch taxes: www.belastingdienst.nl
▶ IDW: www.idw.nl

Money
Matters

Social Security

If you legally reside and/or work in the Netherlands, you are (in principle) subject to the Dutch social security system. So is your partner/spouse and/or other members of your family. However, you may be exempt under EC Regulation 883/2004 or a bilateral social security treaty – this depends on your situation, contract, etc.

There are two kinds of compulsory social insurance schemes in the Netherlands; one that is applicable to the population in general (national insurance schemes) and one that is applicable to employees only (employee insurance schemes).

The National Insurance Schemes

There are five national insurance schemes (*volksverzekeringen*):

General Old Age Pensions Act (AOW): an old age pension paid out upon reaching the age of 65+.

General Surviving Relatives Act (ANW): an income-dependent widow's, widower's or 'dependent children' benefit.

Long-Term Care Act (WLZ): for those who need intensive care or supervision 24/7.

The Health Insurance Act (ZVW): this act determines that everyone who legally resides in the Netherlands and is subject to the Dutch social security system is obligated to have health insurance.

Child Benefit Act (AKW - Kinderbijslag): a benefit paid out to parents who have children under the age of 18.

Contributions (Payable to Tax Department)
Contributions for the national insurance schemes are levied on income up to approximately 33,600 euros a year, together with the income tax.

Employee Insurance Schemes

There are four employee insurance schemes (*werknemersverzekeringen*).

WULBZ / WVLBZ / ZW (In case of illness): based on this act, your employer is obligated to continue paying a percentage of your salary during the first 104 weeks of sickness.

Work and Income According to Labor Capacity Act (WIA): created for those who have been disabled for work for more than 104 weeks. The aim of this act is to stimulate 'ability' for work.

Disability Insurance Act (WAO): for employees who were already receiving the WAO-benefit on January 1, 2006.

Unemployment Insurance Act (WW): an insurance against the financial consequences of unemployment.

Contributions (Payable to Tax Department)
The contributions for the employee insurance schemes are levied by the tax department, together with the wage tax.

Exceptions
EU/EEA/Switzerland
You are not subject to the Dutch social security legislation if you have been posted from another EU or EEA (European Economic

Area) member state or Switzerland, or if you work here shorter than six months. This changes if your income earned in the Netherlands is subject to wage tax here, and you in fact carry out your work here.

There is a whole set of rules surrounding continued coverage of the social insurance system of another EU/EEA/Swiss country; but they are too detailed to go into here. For more information, visit www.belastingdienst.nl, under *Payroll Taxes*.

Non-EU/EE/Switzerland

If the Netherlands has entered into a social security treaty with the country from which you have been posted, this treaty determines which applicable social security legislation applies to you. If you are here temporarily, you will probably continue to be covered by the social security system of the country from which you have been posted.

If you have been posted from a country with which the Netherlands has not entered into a social security treaty, it is – in general – not possible to obtain an exemption from the Dutch social security system.

Taxes

Yes, taxes are high in the Netherlands. But these taxes are not used to support King Louis XVI's life in Versailles, or to expand upon King Charles I's art collection. Instead, a lot of them go right back into our own pockets.

As soon as your child is born, you receive a quarterly amount to help you pay for their needs. And, once your child turns 18, this quarterly amount stops, but no need to worry: he/she can now request a monthly payment – a gift – that amounts to more than the initial benefit. As for higher education; the vast majority of university studies cost a modest 2,000 euros a year in tuition. And, if you can't afford your health insurance, which is already a lot cheaper than in most other countries, the government will help you out. Also if you can't afford to pay your rent, you can ask the government for their support. Plus, there is a multitude of other benefits and government support measures, as well as tax deductions that you can benefit from.

So, that is where a lot of your tax money goes.

Resident Taxpayer

How is it determined whether you owe taxes, and how much you owe? The first question that has to be answered is: are you a resident taxpayer or not? The answer to this is found by evaluating the following points: where do you have your home, where does your family/partner live, where do you work, how long have you lived in the country, what other ties do you have with it?

Tax Boxes

If, based on the above, it is determined that you are a resident taxpayer, then you owe taxes over your entire worldwide income, wherever you earn it (tax treaties may determine differently). There are three 'boxes' over which taxes are due: income from real estate, benefits, shareholding, etc.; income from substantial shareholding; and income from savings and investments.

Tax Rates

Box 1: In this box, there are four tax brackets, divided into approximately 0–20,000 euros (taxed at 37 percent); 20,000–33,600 euros (taxed at 41 percent); 33,600–57,600 euros (also taxed at 41 percent); and more than 57,600 euros (taxed at 52 percent) (tax percentages are approximate, as they change annually, at least behind the comma).

Box 2: taxed at 25 percent.

Box 3: taxed at 30 percent over 4 percent of the assets, creating an effective tax rate of 1.2 percent.

Partners

Taxpayers who (these conditions are not cumulative):

- ▶ Are married or registered partners
- ▶ Have a civil partnership agreement drawn by a civil law notary, including a 'mutual care stipulation'
- ▶ Have a child together
- ▶ Jointly own their main residence
- ▶ Are considered partners in a pension scheme
- ▶ Are considered partners for tax purposes.

Can allocate common sources of income and deductible items – such as mortgage interest for the principal place of residence, medical expenses or study costs – to each other's tax return in such a way that they can reap the maximum benefit from them.

Non-Resident Taxpayer

As a non-resident taxpayer, you only pay income tax on income from certain sources in the Netherlands, such as: Dutch business income, employment income, income from real estate in the Netherlands and income in the form of periodic benefits, and a substantial shareholding in a Dutch company. In most cases, employment income that you earn while you are physically not in the Netherlands is not taxed here.

Partial Non-Resident Taxpayer

This is only an option if you are benefitting from the so-called 30%-ruling (we'll get back to that). In that case, you are a resident of the Netherlands for income (and deductibles) in box 1, but you are treated as a non-resident in boxes 2 and 3.

'Real' Non-Resident Taxpayer

If you are a non-resident, but you earn your income in the Netherlands and would like to benefit from the available deductibles, then you can choose this option. Be sure you consult a tax advisor before making this decision.

30%-ruling

You can make use of the 30%-ruling tax facility if you have been posted from or recruited outside the Netherlands to work in the Netherlands. For this, you do not need to be a resident of the Netherlands and you do not have to (physically) carry out work here, either. The ruling allows your employer to pay you a tax-free allowance of up to 30 percent of your wage for so-called 'extraterritorial expenses' – expenses you would not have had, had you not been sent/placed abroad – as a result of which the effective rate of wage tax is reduced.

There are further conditions that must be met for this – your tax consultant can tell you more.

Double Taxation

As mentioned earlier, you may find yourself owing double taxes. In order to help you avoid this, several countries have entered into tax treaties with each other. In keeping with most of them, you do not owe taxes over income from employment in the Netherlands if:

▶ You are in the Netherlands for, in total 183 days (approximately six months) in any 12-month period or in a fiscal year, and
▶ Your wages are paid by or on behalf of an employer who is not a resident of the Netherlands, and
▶ Your wages are not borne by a permanent establishment or permanent representative of the employer in the Netherlands.

For countries with which the Netherlands has not entered into a tax treaty, there is a unilateral arrangement. This will often mean that income earned abroad is exempt from taxation in the Netherlands, although it will be taken into account for the purpose of calculating the (progressive) tax rate applicable to your further income, which is then taxed in keeping with the 'normal' rules.

Website

▶ Dutch Tax Office:: www.belastingdienst.nl

Health Care Insurance

You cannot legally reside in the Netherlands without medical insurance. So let's get you started on figuring it out.

To pay for health care insurance, everyone pays a fixed contribution to the insurance company and an income-dependent contribution to the tax authorities. This income-dependent contribution is compensated by your employer, who pays it directly to the tax authorities. If you receive a benefit or old age pension, it depends on your social security institution or pension plan whether your income-dependent contribution is compensated.

Health care insurance is free for children under the age of 18

If you are unemployed or self-employed, you receive no compensation. You receive an annual preliminary assessment for the amount you owe, which is based on what the tax authorities estimate you will be earning that year. If you end up paying too much, you will be reimbursed after the final tax assessment over the year in question.

The government offers financial assistance (called *zorgtoeslag*) to persons (also self-employed) whose income lies below a certain level, to help pay the health care insurance premium

Deductible

There is a fixed deductible (see further on); by increasing the amount of the deductible, you can decrease the income-independent part of your contribution. It does not apply to children until the age of 18, visits to the GP, visits to the midwife, maternity care, care covered by voluntary additional insurance or dental care for children/persons until the age of 21.

Selecting an Insurance Company

All insurance companies are obligated to accept all applications, regardless of age, gender or health. The cost of a basic insurance is pretty much the same across the board; doing a little comparative shopping becomes worth your while if you are interested in additional coverage – or eliminating certain coverage. However, insurance companies are not obligated to take you on for additional coverage and can refuse you additional health care insurance.

You can change insurance companies every year. Issues to look at when doing comparative shopping are: the amount of the deductible, coverage while abroad, level of dental care offered, alternative therapies, etc.

Types of Policies

When you are arranging your insurance, you will run into the terms 'natura polis' or 'restitutie polis'.

▶ If you take out a *natura* policy, your insurance company will pay your medical bills directly if you went to a medical service provider with whom they have entered into a contract with (you are free to select your own *huisarts*, or GP). If you visit a specialist/therapist with whom no such contract exists, they will only cover a portion of the expenses.
▶ The *restitutie* policy is slightly more expensive, but does give you freedom of choice as to whom you wish to turn to for medical assistance. Often you pay the bill yourself and then submit it with your insurance company for restitution.

▶ Some insurance companies offer a combination of the two types of insurances, and with many insurance companies you will find they are not excessively strict about the existence of an actual contract between them and the care provider, provided he/she is recognized by a professional organization.

Long-Term Medical Care

The WLZ (Wet Langdurige Ziektekosten, or Long-Term Medical Care Act) is a national insurance scheme that insures persons against risks that cannot be covered by individual insurance. Everyone who legally resides and works in the Netherlands has a right to coverage by this insurance. It is meant to cover steep medical expenses. You owe a contribution for this insurance over income from (self-)employment.

Dental Care

Dental care is not included in any basic package (with the exception of dental care for children up to the age of 18 and 'specialist' dental care, including dentures). Braces are usually covered up to a certain percentage.

Medication

In your policy you are likely to find something along the lines of "we only cover GVS medication". This refers to the fact that types of medication have been 'clustered', after which a maximum price has been determined for this cluster. If you are prescribed medication, then the cluster-specific maximum price is covered by the insurance. If your medication is more expensive than that, you will have to pay the difference.

Check with your insurance company whether you can take out an additional policy to cover these extra costs as well as the cost of homeopathic/alternative medication.

Pregnancy and Childbirth

Visits to your midwife are covered by your insurance, as are at least two ultrasounds, if they are medically required.

Home child birth is covered by your insurance. The costs of a hospital delivery are fully covered if it has been determined that, for health and safety reasons, the baby should be delivered in the hospital. If you voluntarily choose to have your baby in the hospital (called a *poliklinische bevalling*), you might have to contribute towards the costs of your hospital delivery. For more, see *Nine Truths and Myths About Pregnancy*.

Students

If you are a student, your host institution might already have arranged insurance for you – though you should verify this, of course. Special packages for students are available. If you have an EU Health Insurance Card, which you can get if you are insured under the (public) health care scheme in your (EU) home country and your stay abroad is temporary, you will continue to be covered by this insurance policy. It is up to your health insurance provider to determine what constitutes a temporary stay if you go abroad to study. Once you start working on the side, you may have to check if there are any further conditions.

Website

▶ Health care insurance shopping: www.zorgwijzer.nl/ zorgvergelijker/english

A Place to Stay

Renting a Home

You might find yourself unpleasantly surprised by rental prices in the Netherlands, but it is worth realizing that, compared to prices elsewhere in Europe, they are quite reasonable. What might be more of a surprise, are the modest sizes of the apartments and the steep stairs leading up to them – or to the other stories in your house.

Types of Rental Properties
Basically, there are three different types of property you can rent:

▶ Unfurnished (*Ongemeubileerd*). Or empty; no carpeting, no curtains, often a minimum of or no appliances and no utilities.
▶ Semi-furnished (*Gestoffeerd*). Some furnishings and carpeting, and possibly a few appliances. Do ask for a complete list of what is included. Utility inclusion or exclusion depends on the landlord.
▶ Furnished (*Gemeubileerd*). Everything has been taken care of and the apartment is ready to be moved into. It may contain any combination of furniture, appliances, curtains, light fixtures, carpets, cutlery and dishes, television, stereo equipment, kitchen appliances such as microwave, dishwasher, refrigerator, and sometimes even bed linens and blankets or down feather beds. Once again, ask for a complete inventory list before agreeing to anything. If anything is missing, negotiate it before you sign the lease. Utilities are (usually) included.

Many rental contracts have been especially designed to meet the needs of expatriates, and include an English translation

The Rental Contract
A rental contract usually includes the following items:
▶ Rent: payable one month in advance
▶ A deposit: usually one month, sometimes 2 or 3

- An annual adjustment of the rent, based on increases in the cost of living, as determined by the Central Bureau of Statistics (CBS)
- User's costs, such as utilities, municipal levies and garden maintenance
- Diplomatic clause, see the next paragraph
- Brokerage fee
- A clause on minor repairs
- A clause stating that the lessee is responsible for the yearly cleaning of the central heating system, water boilers, chimneys, gutters and draining pipes
- The obligation to return the property in the same condition, normal wear and tear excepted, at the end of the rental period – or else forfeit (a part of) the deposit.

Generally, regardless of the cause of the damage, the lessee pays 200 euros, excl. VAT, per case. All costs of larger repairs, external or internal, which are not due to any fault of the lessee, are paid by the owner.

Diplomatic Clause

It *can* happen, that you have rented a property, but are sent to another location or country before the rental contract comes to its end – or that the owner, who rented it out to you because he himself was sent abroad, is brought back home by his employer. In these situations, one of you will have to able to terminate the rental contract before the agreed term is over. In order to be able to do this, make sure you include a diplomatic clause in your rental contract, which gives either of you the option of terminating the contract after a notification term mutually agreed upon in advance, should this be necessary.

A verbal contract is binding under Dutch law. Therefore, unless you are absolutely sure you will take the property, do not make any written *or* verbal commitment!

Checking In

Once you have signed the contract and been handed over the keys, you are checked in by the owner or his representative, assisted by his own agent. A checklist is filled out regarding the condition of the house, the furniture, fixtures and fittings belonging to the house, the condition of the exterior/garden, and the inventory. The house should be thoroughly cleaned, including the inside of kitchen and bathroom cabinets. The inspection report as well as the inventory list must be signed by the lessee and the lessor.

Do a careful walk-through of the house or apartment you are planning on renting, to verify existing damages and the need for repairs and improvements. Put in writing who will be responsible for arranging and paying for these repairs, etc., before you sign on the dotted line.

Terminating the Rental Contract

If you do not specifically stipulate in writing that, after the initial one-year rental period, you will vacate the premises, the contract undergoes a *stilzwijgende verlenging* or silent continuance. This means you will be liable for a new year of rental fees and you will at the very least forfeit your deposit (usually two months' rent) if you move out anyway.

If, after the initial one-year period, you want to continue your lease on a month-to-month basis, this can be negotiated, depending on your landlord. Or you might opt to to continue your rental contract for a longer period of time. Either agreement should be confirmed in writing.

Always inform (remind) your landlord well in advance regarding when the contract for your apartment will expire and when you will be leaving, by registered letter. Depending on your rental contract, the notice period will be:

▶ At least one calendar month for you (the lessee)
▶ At least three months + one month for every year the property has been rented if your landlord terminates the contract.

Checking Out

Usually on the last day, an official check-out will take place, checking the inventory and condition of the lease property with the checklist made when you moved in. If the state of the property is found to be satisfactory and all bills in connection with the property have been paid, the deposit will be paid back within three months after the check-out date. If necessary, the costs of restoring the rental property back to the required state will be deducted from the deposit in accordance with the bills provided by the lessor.

Taxes

There is no tax facility for renting a house. If your employer chooses to compensate you for the housing costs, this will be considered taxable income if you are a (partial non-) resident taxpayer. Whether you will have to pay the tax yourself depends on whether your contract is net or gross.

If you benefit from the 30%-ruling, a part of the rent may be qualified as an 'extraterritorial expense' (you can read more about this in the chapter on *Taxes*). That part of the rent can be compensated free of tax.

If you are a non-resident of the Netherlands, any compensation of double housing expenses is considered compensation for extraterritorial expenses: tax-free, but resulting in a reduction of the 30%-allowance.

Buying a Home

Real Estate Agent

Though you can go a long way on your own with the help of the Internet, we advise you to contact an agent for the actual house-search and negotiation phase. Besides the fact that they have access to a computerized multiple-listing system which keeps them completely up-to-date on properties available in their district, they are familiar with the price ranges, local contracts, 'invisible' obligations, laws and customs, as well as the local bidding systems, zoning plans (*bestemmingsplan*), soil contamination and city council regulations.

Real estate agents charge a brokerage fee (*courtage*) for their services of approximately 1 to 2 percent of the purchase price of the house, though it can be negotiable. Some offer an expat service package.

There are 417,000 unoccupied houses in the Netherlands

Advantages and Disadvantages of Buying

Aside from the fact that the value of your house might go up by the time you sell it, there are a number of other advantages as well:

► You get a tax relief on the mortgage interest if the house is your principal place of residence, provided you take out an annuity or straight line mortgage.

► A number of the costs related to the financing of the house are also tax-deductible, such as: some of the civil law notary's fees, the closing commission, and the fee for the appraisal of the house.

Disadvantages are:

► You pay approximately 6 percent of the purchase price as one-time buyers' expenses. These expenses consist of a transfer tax, estate agent fees, civil law notary's fees, a fixed fee for the bank or broker, etc.
► You must add the so-called deemed rental value (*eigenwoningforfait* – we'll get back to this) to your taxable income and pay taxes over this.

Points to Keep in Mind
► Once you have a real estate agent, ask him to advise you on matters such as environmental laws, the survey of the house, hidden defects, and issues surrounding leasehold vs. free-hold.
► The purchase price excludes furniture, carpets, curtains, light fixtures and sometimes kitchen appliances. You can negotiate which goods could be included in the purchase.
► You pay a deposit of approximately 10 percent of the purchase price of the house which is due approximately five weeks after the deal has been made. It is to be paid to a civil law notary and can be part of the financing agreement reached for the purchase of the house.
► If you will be taking out a mortgage, make sure the purchase agreement is subject to financing.
► Other resolutive conditions can be included, such as being able to obtain a permit to occupy the real estate, or even more importantly, the option of having a constructional survey carried out.

If you need the assistance of an interpreter when communicating with the civil law notary, you are legally required to request the assistance of a sworn interpreter. Depending on your language, this will cost you anywhere between 150 and 500 euros.

Find out whether your house is a 'monument'. If it is, you will be subject to strict rules regarding maintenance, painting and reconstruction.

What Type of Mortgage?

You should seek proper advice on the type of mortgage that is suitable in your situation, particularly in view of the limited period of time during which you may need the mortgage. Do not forget to inform the bank if you are benefiting from the 30%-ruling. If you come here as an actual expat, the two major tax issues with which you will be faced are the 30%-ruling and the choice between resident and partial non-resident tax status. Be sure to get expert advice!

Deemed Rental Value and WOZ-Value

Those who own a house and use it as their principal place of residence have to report a certain amount – related to the home ownership – on their income tax return. This amount is a percentage of the value of the house, and is called the *eigenwoningforfait* (or deemed rental value). The *eigenwoningforfait* is based on the official value of the house, also known as the WOZ-value, which is determined every year by the municipality.

Preliminary Tax Refund

The balance of the deemed rental value and the interest can be deducted from your income. You can receive a tax refund on the mortgage interest deduction every month by requesting a preliminary negative tax bill from the tax authorities. The tax authorities will then deposit the refund directly into your bank account.

Local Taxes

If you own a home, you will also find yourself paying local, municipal taxes. These will amount to approximately 2,000 euros a year.

Exemption from Customs Duties

If you transfer goods from a non EU-country to an EU-Member State (such as the Netherlands), you are subject to customs duties, VAT and other special taxes (for example excises and a special tax on cars). A special exemption can provide relief in these circumstances if you meet certain conditions.

Usually your removal company can take care of the related administrative obligations.

When looking for a contractor, visit the BouwGarant website. Under *vind een aannemer bij jou in de buurt* (find a contractor nearby you) you fill in the name of your municipality or your postal code. Be sure to invite a few contractors, as prices can vary considerably.

Websites

▶ Looking for a house: www.funda.nl, www.jaap.nl, www.zah.nl, www.pararius.nl

▶ Contractors: www.bouwgarant.nl

The Process of Buying a House

▶ You select a real estate agent, and discuss what you are looking for, what you need and what is realistic.

▶ If you have any special wishes regarding the property, make sure your real estate agent and the real estate agent of the seller are aware of this. If they are not, and it turns out your home does not meet these wishes, you cannot hold them accountable for it.

▶ You contact a mortgage provider, to find out exactly how much mortgage you can take out, whereby you take into account additional expenses involved in the purchase of the home (these are discussed further on).

▶ You visit property.

▶ When you have found a home you like, be sure to discuss all issues such as city council regulations, but also issues such as soil contamination.

▶ If you want this home, you can inform your real estate agent of this verbally.

▶ Your real estate agent will contact the selling party and relay this message.

▶ Have a building inspection carried out. If you fail to do this and there is a problem, more likely than not, you will have lost your right to hold the seller accountable.

▶ Make the purchase of the house contingent upon its passing the building inspection.

▶ The initial verbal agreement you reach with the seller is put in writing in the preliminary purchase contract. A penalty clause is usually included in case the seller or the buyer does not meet his obligations.

▶ After being signed by all the parties, the preliminary purchase contract is sent to the civil law notary who deals with the transfer of the title of the house.

▶ A three-day 'cooling-off' period starts the day after the buyer receives a copy of the signed contract. During these three days the buyer can cancel the deal without any repercussions and without having to state the reason.

▶ The civil law notary inspects the public registers of the Land Registry regarding mortgages and/or attachments with which the property may be encumbered.

▶ The transfer of ownership takes place at the civil law notary's office by means of a deed of transfer that is drawn up by the civil law notary and signed by the seller, the buyer and the civil law notary. You will receive a draft of this deed and of the mortgage deed beforehand. Also your agent will receive these and check them.

- The agent will check together with you to see whether the house has been vacated, and is in the agreed condition.
- The civil law notary takes care of the financial settlement of the transaction and ensures that the deed of transfer is entered in the public registers (Land Registry).
- The transfer then becomes official and you receive the keys of your new house.

Setting Up House – Monthly Expenses

When you have bought your home, there are a number of things you will be wanting to arrange, such as utilities, telephone, TV, insurances and, while your at it, let's start with a bank account.

Bank Account

To open a bank account, you first have to decide which bank you want to work with. In alphabetical order, you will probably consider the following banks: ABN Amro, ING, Rabobank, SNS, Triodos – though there are more! Next, you visit the bank's website to make an appointment at a bank office, or you can set up a bank account on-line. In both cases, someone from the bank call you, either to inform you on what you need to bring, or else to help you set up a bank account after verifying your data. Once this has been arranged, you will receive a debit card, with an activation code and a pin code, by mail. You can use the debit card to make payments in stores, with the use of your pin code.

Insurance

You can arrange your house-related (as well as other) insurances via the same bank: home insurance and household contents insurance, but also legal liability and valuables. The cost is calculated based on where you live, what you insure, what it would cost to rebuild your house, and your deductible. You pay a fixed amount, per 1,000

euros of insured value. A home contents insurance will cost you between 9 and 17 euros a month and once again mostly depends on the insured value and where you live.

Liability insurance covers any damage you, or your children, cause to other persons or their property. Insuring 1,000,000 euros, with no deductible, starts at 2.70 euros a month, for a single person, and starts at 4.65 per month for a family with children. It is a modest monthly premium to pay for accidents that, as the Dutch say, 'lie in a small corner' (meaning: small mishaps can have big consequences).

Utilities

A substantial amount of your income will go to utilities – gas and electricity. Shop around to determine which company offers you the best rates, because they tend to vary. In most cases, they determine how much they think you will have to pay them on a monthly basis, depending on whether you live in an apartment, a detached house, a semi-detached house, a house on a corner of a row of houses, or a house in the middle of a row of houses – and how many people live in your household. They will send you this estimate, and if you want, you can lower or raise it online. If you pay too much, they return it to you (and make a new, lower, estimate for the next year) and if you pay too little, you are presented with an additional bill (and a new estimate). Other factors taken into account are where you live, and for how long you take out the contract. The cost varies from approximately 70 euros, for one person in an apartment, to 210 euros for four persons in a detached house – though plenty of people end up paying a whole lot more than 210 euros! It depends, of course, on how resistant you are to the persistent cold of the Dutch winters.

So-called 'green' – or 'sustainable' energy is also available. You can find companies that supply this on the site of the Consumers' Association (www.consumentenbond.nl).

Water

For the water you use, you pay an amount to your local water supplier. For a four-person household, this will amount to approximately 20 euros a month.

Local Taxes

Another goodly amount of your income will go to local taxes: waste collection tax, municipal property tax, water board assessments, sewerage charges, etc. Some of these charges are fixed, others are calculated based on the value of your home. As a renter, you only owe a fixed (the amount of which depends on whether you are living alone or with a family) amount for waste collection.

If your house is worth 300,000 euros, you will owe approximately 680 euros a year in municipal taxes. If it is worth 750,000, you will owe approximately 1,120 euros.

Telephone and Television

A combined subscription for telephone and television will cost you between 32 and 82 euros month, depending on the MBs involved and any additional features, such as television-on-demand, HBO, etc.

A Car

The monthly expenses involved in having a car in the Netherlands include not only, obviously, gasoline and insurance, but also Road Tax (*motorrijtuigenbelasting*). The amount depends on the weight of your car, the province you live in, the type of fuel, etc. and, for the average car, will range from 33 to 47 euros.

If you own a car or a motorcycle, you are legally required to take out *Wettelijke aansprakelijkheidsverzekering*, or *WA-verzekering*, to cover any damage you cause to another person or person's property. You can also insure damage to your own car, in which case you can choose between *beperkt casco* and *volledig casco* (or all-risk). *Volledig casco* includes damage caused by an 'outside force', such as fire, theft, storm, slipping on ice, collision, etc. – even if it is your fault that this 'outside force' impacted your car. With *beperkt casco*, you are not covered for damage that you have caused yourself, yet you *are* covered for fire, theft, storm, a collision with an animal, and glass breakage. The price of car insurance varies, depending on the level of coverage you opt for – as well as where you live, the type of car, how many claim-free years you accumulate over time, etc. The average car insurance costs approximately 92 euros a month.

A Cell Phone
You can take out a monthly subscription with a cell phone or buy a separate phone and take out a so-called sim-only subscription. Or you take out a pre-paid subscription. The cheapest sim-only subscriptions start around 11 euros, the cheapest subscriptions start at 10 euros, but you add a certain amount depending how much you decide to pay up-front for the phone. The cheapest pre-paid subscription will get you 10 euros worth of 10-cent-a-minute calls, or 10-cent-a-text messages. Once you add MBs, this will bring you up to 16 euros a month, in combination with above rates.

Energy Label

For quite a while now, cars and household equipment have been issued an 'energy label', ranging from A–G, to indicate how energy-efficient they are. A is the most efficient, G the least. All houses/apartments must also carry this same label (also called *energieprestatiecertificaat*), to be issued by a certified advisor, which is valid for a period of ten years and is handed over with the sale or renting out of the house/apartment. If you cannot show this label, you will not be able to sell your house, while renters will owe less rent. This is all part of the government's aim to become one of the cleanest and most energy-efficient countries within Europe. Measures that influence the classification of your house are, for instance: roof insulation, double glazing, and a ventilation that allows the recuperation of heat. Though you are not obligated to take measures to improve the rating of your house, doing so may contribute to increasing its value, while you might be able to get a more favorable mortgage.

On January 2010, a new type of energy label was introduced, that takes into account the type of house and that provides more information on how energy can be saved, making it easier to compare the energy efficiency of houses, and in 2015, all homeowners in the Netherlands were issued a provisional label, aimed at encouraging them to look into how they can upgrade their energy efficiency. Anyone who wants to sell or rent out their house, will first have to arrange a definitive label – or risk a 450-euro fine.

The cost of obtaining the energy label costs depends on the size and type of house. In the case of apartment buildings, a rebate may be possible, while, in the case of 'similar houses' an 'example house' of the series may be used as a basis. Nonetheless, a separate certificate must be issued for each house. A certified advisor can be found by visiting www.energielabelvoorwoningen.nl, and following the steps on this site. You will need your Digid (or digital identity) to do this. As the site is in Dutch, you might wish to enlist the assistance of your realtor to arrange the energy label.

Education

Should You Choose an International Education or 'Go Dutch'?

Before enrolling your child at a school, you'll have to decide whether to send them to an international school or 'go Dutch'. Both have their own advantages, which you can read about here.

Length of Stay in the Netherlands

If you are planning to stay in the Netherlands for a short period, an international school may provide your child with a greater sense of continuity.

If you are planning on staying for a longer period, and would like your child to mix with the local culture and learn the Dutch language, you may prefer to choose a Dutch school.

Your Child's Age

Another factor to consider is your child's age. In the first two years of Dutch school (ages 4–6), the focus is on learning through play, Dutch language acquisition, social and motor skills, and gradual preparation for reading and writing. 4 and 5-year-olds who don't speak Dutch can usually start a regular Dutch school straight away. They normally pick up the language quickly and are (almost) fluent before formal reading and writing starts at age 6.

Foreign children aged 6 and older are usually required to follow a Dutch immersion program before starting regular school. This takes about one year, after which they can continue their education with children of the same age at a Dutch school.

Difference in Cost

The third factor is the huge difference in cost. Apart from a few private, fee-paying schools, all Dutch schools (primary, secondary and tertiary institutions) are government-funded. Parents pay a small contribution with which the schools pay for a few extra things.

Some international schools are partly subsidized by the Dutch government, while others are completely private. For a subsidized school, the annual fees are about 5,500 euros per child, while for private international schools they are at least 12,000 euros a year.

Curriculums

A unique feature of the Dutch school system is the choice in type of education. Among the state-funded schools there are some religious schools (Catholic, Protestant, Christian, Islamic, Jewish) or those that follow specific philosophic or pedagogic principles (e.g. Montessori, Waldorf). All schools are obligated to adhere to the government's 'core objectives', which specify what all pupils in all schools need to accomplish each year. The individual schools may fill in the specific details.

You'll also find some schools with a bilingual curriculum (usually Dutch and English). These schools vary in the amount of time they teach in English, and usually require a child aged 6 or older to have a decent level of Dutch, before they can join classes with Dutch-speaking peers.

International schools normally either follow the curriculum of the country they are related to, or use the innovative, theme-based International Primary Curriculum (IPC). A few international primary schools make use of the inquiry-based International Baccalaureate (IBPYP) program. As this program is expensive, many international schools only follow the IPC program in primary years, and then the Middle Years Program (MYP) and Diploma Program (DP) in secondary years.

Holidays

The Dutch school attendance law is very strict. From age 5, your child is only allowed to miss school for very specific reasons, e.g. a family emergency or important celebration. International schools are often a bit more flexible in allowing their pupils to take time off during term time, although absences due to extended holidays or early departures at holiday times are usually strongly discouraged.

The summer holiday in Dutch schools lasts six weeks. During the school year, there is at least one week of holiday after each period of about six weeks, so that both pupils and teachers can recharge their batteries. International schools either follow the holiday periods of the country they are related to, or set their own schedule. Pupils at international schools usually enjoy longer summer breaks than their Dutch peers, but often don't have the frequent breaks throughout the year, and their school days are normally longer.

Foreign Families in Dutch Schools

Contrary to international schools, most Dutch primary schools don't give homework till the higher classes. This means that, as a non-Dutch speaking parent, you won't need to worry much about not being able to help your child with homework. As the schools' approach and experience with non-Dutch families differs greatly, it is always good to find out about this before you choose a school.

Secondary Education

At Dutch schools, the pupils take the 'Central End Test for Primary Education' in the last year of primary school (ages 11 or 12). This is a standardized aptitude test with questions testing their Dutch language and comprehension skills, mathematics, study skills, and (optionally) world orientation.

Before this test takes place, the teacher assesses what level of secondary school education (see below) would fit each pupil best. They base their recommendation on various factors including the pupil's test scores from lower classes, intelligence, attitude towards learning, eagerness to learn and interests. The assessment of the teacher is the deciding factor.

Insufficient Dutch language skills can negatively impact a child's secondary school recommendation. If a child is motivated to improve their Dutch, and wants to attend a higher school level than their recommendation, there is the option of attending a one-year *Kopklas*, focused on the Dutch language. At the end of *Kopklas*, the child will hopefully get a recommendation for a higher school level than they had the previous year.

The different types of secondary schools, from lowest to highest academic ability, are as follows:

- ▶ **VMBO** – preparatory secondary vocational education: 4 years, followed by MBO (Intermediate Vocational Education)
- ▶ **HAVO** – senior general secondary education: 5 years, followed by HBO (Hogeschool/University of Applied Sciences)
- ▶ **VWO** – pre-university education: 6 years, followed by (research-oriented) university (= WO)

Many secondary schools have a mixed-level 'bridge class' in the 1st year. Secondary education generally continues till the ages of 16-18, depending on the level. After obtaining a diploma from one level (for example HAVO), you may proceed to the next level (VWO). Likewise, after completing HBO you may continue to university. For some university courses in the Netherlands, you can only enroll if you have followed a particular program during the last years of secondary school, for example Culture & Society, Economics & Society, Nature & Health, and Nature & Technology.

Most universities worldwide accept students with a VWO diploma. Sometimes they have additional requirements, for example proficiency in the local language and/or having passed the VWO exam with high grades. Higher education is offered at a high standard in the Netherlands; all 13 state-funded Dutch universities score well in The Times Higher Education World University Rankings.

International Secondary Education
International schools at secondary level often offer the IBMYP (ages 11–16) and IBDP (ages 16–19) curriculums. The IBDP is a globally-recognized high standard diploma, valued at the same level as a Dutch VWO diploma, and gives access to a research-oriented university. It is possible that a Dutch university requires proof of Dutch language proficiency, and/or a pass in a certain subject examined at secondary level. However, there are plenty of courses at Dutch universities that are completely in English.

Difficulties might arise when an international student is not capable of performing at this high level. International schools usually don't offer their subjects at a lower level and international students often don't speak Dutch well enough to continue their education at a Dutch school. Also, although the IBMYP program could be compared with HAVO, most Universities for Applied Sciences (HBO) don't value the former as highly, since a diploma is not awarded at the end of the MYP.

---

40 percent of the population between 25 and 34 have a higher education degree; 37 percent of men and 44 percent of women)

Websites
▶ www.New2nl.com
▶ eseng.nl – special education needs
▶ www.sio.nl – list of all international schools

Going to University

The higher education system in the Netherlands is based on a three-cycle degree system, consisting of a bachelor's, master's and PhD degree. It is offered at two types of institutions: research universities (WO) and universities of applied sciences (HBO). Research universities primarily offer research-oriented programs, and universities of applied sciences offer programs of higher professional education, which prepare students for specific professions. They tend to be more practice-oriented than the programs offered by research universities.

'Research' Universities
Academic education universities (*universiteit*) are organized around a bachelor's or undergraduate phase that lasts three years and a master's or graduate phase that lasts one to two years. An overview of English-language university studies can be found on the website

listed below. As many Dutch universities have partner institutions in other EU countries, students can follow part of their course abroad. Visit www.studyfinder.nl for international study programs.

Hogescholen or 'Universities of Applied Sciences'

HBO (*Hoger Beroepsonderwijs*, or higher professional education) focuses on applied arts and sciences in one of the seven HBO sectors: agriculture, engineering and technology, economics and business administration, health care, fine and performing arts, education/teacher training, and social welfare.

The universities of applied sciences offer four-year bachelor's degree programs as well as master's programs lasting one to two years. All degree programs focus on preparing students for particular professions and are more practically-oriented, often requiring students to complete an internship or work placement (*stage*).

International Education

Next to the research universities and universities of applied sciences, Holland has a third and smaller branch of higher education, officially known as 'International Education' (IE), which offers advanced training courses, taught in English, originally designed for people from developing countries whose jobs require highly specialized knowledge. Most of the IE institutions are part of a research university and focus on courses relevant to developing countries.

Requirements for Admission

For access to WO bachelor's programs, students are required to have an IB-diploma, a VWO-diploma or to have completed the first year (60 ECTS, see further on) of an HBO program. The minimum access requirement for HBO is an IB-diploma (and, in some cases, the IGCSE-diploma with two additional subjects at GCE-level), the Dutch HAVO/VWO-diploma or a level-4 MBO-diploma.

A quota, or *numerus fixus*, applies for access to certain programs, primarily in the health sector, and places are allocated using a weighted lottery. Potential students older than 21 years of age who do not possess one of the qualifications mentioned above can qualify for access to higher education on the basis of an entrance examination and assessment. The only access requirement for the Open University is that applicants be at least 18 years of age.

To determine whether your diploma qualifies, if you have a non-Dutch secondary school-diploma or an IB-diploma, you must have your diploma evaluated by your prospective educational institute

---

Doctorate

All research universities in the Netherlands are entitled to award a PhD. The process by which a doctorate is obtained is referred to as the *promotie* and the minimum amount of time required to complete a doctorate is four years.

Candidates with foreign qualifications may apply for these positions and ask for permission to write their dissertation in another language. You can also contact a university faculty independently, and write your own research proposal and sometimes you can conduct the research for a dissertation in your own country.

A number of university centers offer Dutch as a second language-courses. The courses are specially designed for foreign students who have otherwise qualified for admission to Dutch higher education, but must first master the language.

Choosing a University

The Dutch system of quality control guarantees that the education offered at all the institutions meets the same high standards. Instead, students look at which specializations are offered and which emphasis or academic tradition is featured.

To double-check the quality of the institution you are considering, visit the website listed below of the NVAO.

Language

To enroll in a program or course that is conducted in English, you must have the appropriate level of command of the English language. To determine this, you must take an English language test, such as TOEFL or IELTS.

Making the Transition

In order to prepare for studying the Netherlands, there are three additional options. Contact your university to see what options there are for you:

▶ You are allowed come here for a year first to study Dutch.
▶ You can come here for a year to follow a preparatory program for the particular studies of your choice.
▶ A transitional year that has been created for specifically for non-European, non-Western students to help them prepare for their studies here, this is called a *schakeljaar*.

On our following pages: Practical Matters for Incoming Students.

Websites

▶ The Dutch higher education system: www.studyinholland.nl/education-system
▶ English-language studies: www.studyinholland.nl
▶ Quality control: www.nvao.com

Practical Matters for Incoming Students

Tuition

From a tuition point of view, there are two types of institutions of higher education: those that are government-funded and those that are government-approved. Studying at a government-funded institution will cost approximately 2,000 euros a year, for EU/EEA/Swiss/Surinam-students. Students of all other nationalities generally pay higher fees, on average 8,000 euros – though it can go up to upwards of 15,000 euros, depending on the length and level of the program.

Residence Permit

To be granted a residence permit for study purposes, you must follow a study at a recognized school or university (of applied sciences). All Dutch educational institutes must apply for the residence permits on behalf of their foreign students; you are not allowed to do this yourself. They request this at the same time they request an MVV (authorization temporary stay) for you, with which you will be allowed to enter the country. Upon arrival you pick up your residence permit at the IND – as the MVV merely allows you to enter the country and is only valid for 90 days. You will also have to register with the municipality (registration GBA).

If you are an EU/EEA-national, you do not need a residence permit, but if you stay here longer than four months, you need to register with the municipality.

Health Care Insurance

Once you are a resident of the Netherlands, in principle you are obligated to arrange private health insurance (perhaps your host institution has arranged a collective insurance in which you can participate).

If you are under the age of 30 and here solely for the purpose of studying, you do not need to take out Dutch health care insurance. Also, if you are insured under the public health care scheme in your (EU) home country and your stay abroad is temporary, you will probably continue to be covered by this insurance policy. It is up to your health insurance provider to determine what constitutes a temporary stay. You can request an EU Health Insurance Card (EHIC) to prove that you are insured.

Internship/Work Permit

If you have a residence permit for studying in the Netherlands, and you have to do an internship here, you do not need a work permit. You do need to arrange the standard internship agreement.

If you are not studying in the Netherlands, and want to come here to do an internship or to acquire work experience, then if you are a non-EU/EEA/Swiss national, you will need a work permit.

A Job on the Side

As a student, you are allowed to work a maximum of ten hours a week, or full-time during the months of June, July and August. Your employer will need to apply for a work permit. EU/EEA/Swiss students can work as many hours as they like, without the need for a work permit – with the exception of Croatian students, who will need a work permit during their first twelve months on the Dutch labor market.

Finding a Job After Graduating

If you are a graduate of a foreign university, you can come to the Netherlands for a period of three years to find work (as the case may be; as a highly skilled migrant). You can read more about this on our pages on *Work Permit*.

Costs of Daily Living

Your daily expenses will include tuition, rent and daily expenses, as well as basic health insurance, obtaining a permit, transportation (unless you qualify for a public transportation pass, see further on), books, notebooks and perhaps membership fees for student (sports) organizations. You can expect all this to amount to approximately 800 – 1,300 euros a month, though this of course depends on the amount of tuition you owe. Housing will cost you between 300 and 600 euros a month.

Housing

It is hard to find proper housing. If you are participating in an exchange program or are enrolled in an international course, it is quite possible that housing has been arranged for you by the institution. If your institution has not actually arranged housing for you, they often have special departments for foreign students that help them find a suitable place to live.

Once you have found a place to live, what can you expect? In Holland, students usually have their own room. You might have to share the shower, toilet, kitchen and living room with other students, and it is common for men and women to live together in a shared house.

There are a few national and international student organizations that can help you find internships, work placements and temporary jobs, as well as fun and interesting activities. The most important ones are AEGEE and AIESEC.

Finances

Most banks will probably be willing to support you financially and to answer any finance-related questions you may have. Ask about their loans. At least the following banks have special programs for students: ABN Amro, ING, Rabobank and SNS.

If you would like to take on a paid job alongside your studies, you will need a *burgerservicenummer* (BSN, Citizen Service Number). You are issued one automatically when you register with your municipality. If you are a non-EU/EEA/Swiss citizen, you will also need your student residence permit and a work permit. You also need a BSN to arrange health care insurance.

Grants

To find out more about scholarships, also for non-EU students, and whether you qualify, visit www.grantfinder.nl. Here you can enter your field of study and your country of origin and see for which grants or scholarships you might qualify. Also check Scholarship-Portal.eu or contact your university in the Netherlands to find out whether it has a grant for international students, as some have their own grant programs.

Those who have refugee status or are asylum seekers and are starting a higher education can approach Stichting UAF Steunpunt (www.uaf.nl) for more information on the possibilities of a grant.

Studiefinanciering

If you are younger than 30, registered for a full-time or a dual education, and have the same rights as a Dutch national, you can apply for student finance (*studiefinanciering*). *Studiefinanciering* is made up of four elements: a loan, a public transportation card (*OV Studenten chipkaart*), an additional loan and a tuition fee loan (*collegegeldkrediet*). All of these amounts must be paid back, with the exception of the additional loan and the public transportation card, which you will not have to pay back *provided* you obtain your diploma within ten years.

The amounts change annually, but the basic loan lies around slightly more than 860 euros a month; the additional loan depends on your parents' financial situation and is a maximum of approximately 270 euros a month, while the tuition fee loan is approximately 165 euros a month.

More information can be found on the website listed below. There you will also find when you have the 'same rights' as a Dutch national as well as more about limited funding assistance if you do not meet the requirements.

Be sure to arrange a DigiD (your digital identity), in order to arrange your studiefinanciering/tuition fee loan online!

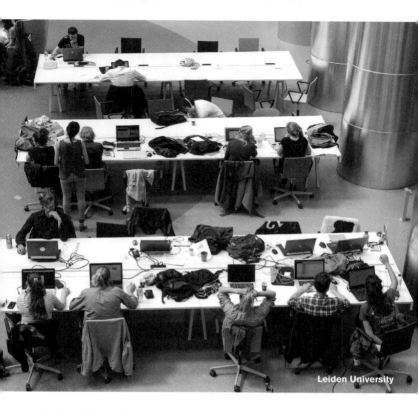

Leiden University

Going Abroad

You can 'take' your *studiefinanciering* abroad with you, subject to conditions you can find on the DUO website.

Websites

► Daily expenses: www.studyinholland.nl/practical-matters/daily-expenses.
► Student finance (*studiefinanciering*): duo.nl/particulier/international-student
► Refugees/asylum seekers: www.uaf.nl

Getting
around

Public Transportation

Trains

The Netherlands has a dense railway network that offers frequent service, as well as the quickest way to travel between city centers. The carriages are modern and clean and, although many Dutch people complain about delays, the trains usually run on time (everything is relative!).

The Dutch trains have first and second class compartments. First class costs about 50 percent more and the seats are slightly larger and less likely to be full. Though smoking and no-smoking compartments are indicated, smoking is no longer allowed on the trains, nor in the halls, stairs, flyovers, elevators or covered platforms. Platforms have a designated smokers' area, indicated by a pillar with an ashtray, a 'smoking' sign and the words *rookzone*.

High Speed Trains

You can travel by high-speed train (the Thalys or the TGV) from Amsterdam, Schiphol or Rotterdam to Belgium and – final destination – Paris. If you are going to Germany or Switzerland, you can take the high-speed ICE train, and if you are going to London, there is the Eurostar. These high-speed trains are really only a worthwhile option if you intend to travel all the way to these far-away destinations as, within the Netherlands, the trains still travel at regular speeds through the densely populated areas. Only once they reach France, do they pick up speed. In other words, don't count on cutting time by taking the high-speed train from Amsterdam to Rotterdam.

You can only travel on a high-speed train if you have bought a special (more expensive) ticket for this train and have made a reservation. If you accidentally board the Thalys in Amsterdam to go visit you friend in Rotterdam and you are caught, you will be fined!

The Public Transportation Card – *OV-Chipkaart*

There two types of public transportation card, or OV-chipkaart: the personal OV-chipkaart and the so-called anonymous OV-chipkaart. The personal OV-chipkaart is a plastic credit-card shaped public transportation card with your photograph that contains information on the amount of credit it still has on it, on whether you have a right to certain reductions, and on whether you are traveling on the basis of a public transportation 'subscription', or pass. You can find travel discount products on www.ov-chipkaart; click on *English*, *Reloading*, and *National Travel Products*.

Tourists can buy an anonymous *OV-chipkaart* or a disposable *OV-chipkaart* at the station (at an NS ticket automat), a supermarket, a newsagent, on the tram/bus, at the airport, or a public transportation company. The anonymous card can be used for more than one day and/or longer distances, the disposable card for a single use or short period.

You can also buy train tickets online, on the site listed below.

Do not forget to load credit onto the *OV-chipkaart* before using it! You can do this at the counter of a public transportation company or at the NS ticket automat at the train station, on one of their yellow devices. It will require a certain minimum amount before it will approve your trip.

Using the OV-Chipkaart

When entering the platform at the train station, you hold your card against the card reader (either a white pole with the dark pink oval that says *Kaart hier*, or a yellow pole with the grey circle and an illustration of the card that says *OV-chipkaart*). When you get off the train and leave the station, you do the same.

In the buses and trams, you hold the card against the card read just inside the door as you go in and as you go out. If you forget to check out, you can visit the website listed below to see if you can fix this.

Students are issued a public transportation pass. You can choose whether you want to travel for free between Monday morning 4 a.m. and Saturday morning 4 a.m. (and at a reduced price during the weekends, on holidays and during summer break) or for free between noon Fridays and Monday 4 a.m., as well as holidays and summer break, and at a reduced price on weekdays. It is considered a loan that you don't have to pay back if you graduate within 10 years. More information can be found on the website listed below.

Even though you use the same pass to travel by train, bus and tram (metro), you need to check out of each one before you get on another one! Largely, this does not apply if you switch trains, but it does apply if you go from traveling by train to say, traveling by bus. When does it apply when traveling by train? When you switch companies: to a regional train company, such as Arriva or Connexxion.

Passes

There are a wide variety of passes and special tickets that can save you money when using public transportation. Which type you choose depends on the kind of traveling you will be doing – frequent or infrequent, long distances or short, alone or in a group, during rush hour or not, and your age. The clerks at the ticket windows can help you make your choice.

You cannot use a credit card to buy an *OV-chipkaart*

Taxis

You cannot hail taxis on the street in the Netherlands like you can in many parts of the world. You must either request one by phone, or go to a taxi-stand where taxis wait. All major railway stations have a taxi-stand. Hotels and restaurants are always happy to call a taxi for you if you ask. The regular Dutch taxis use meters and charge roughly the same rates. When you start, the meter will already show a balance of several euros. This ensures the driver a minimum fare. Only for very long distances is it sometimes possible to negotiate a fare in advance. It is customary to give taxi drivers a tip, which usually means increasing the amount up to a round figure.

There are also regional taxis that you can share with other passengers, thus reducing the cost. On the site listed below, you will find a list of all the regional share taxi companies – the site is in Dutch, however, so just a few tips: you request the taxi an hour in advance, you can expect him to arrive anywhere between 15 minutes earlier and 15 minutes later, you can only travel within the region (20–25 km), you can expect (obviously) other passengers, and you pay approximately 4 euros per 5 km. If you receive a WMO-benefit, you travel at a reduced rate.

Schiphol Taxis

Below you will find a site on taxi services to and from Schiphol Airport, as well as a hotel shuttle for Amsterdam.

Websites

► Information and purchase *OV-chipkaart*: www.ov-chipkaart.nl (click on *English*)
► Online train ticket: www.ns.nl/producten/producten/p/e-ticket
► Students: www.ov-chipkaart.nl/apply-1/which-card-is-right-for-you/students.htm
► Getting to and from the train station: www.ns.nl/en, click on *English*, *Menu*, *Door to Door*
► Traveling with functional disabilities: www.ns.nl/en, click on *English*, *Menu*, *Traveling with a Functional Disability*
► To and from Schiphol Airport: www.schiphol.nl/Travellers/ToFromSchiphol/SchipholTravelTaxi.htm
► Hotel shuttle: www.airporthotelshuttle.nl
► All other airports: www.taxi2airport.nl/en

Cycling

During morning rush hour, the bicycle paths in the big cities become very dangerous as they can barely accommodate the number of cyclists and because these same cyclists are too focused on their cell phones. This is the conclusion of the Association for Scientific Research into traffic safety, based on research carried out in The Hague and Amsterdam.

In both cities, they set up cameras to study what was going on on four different bicycle paths and it became clear that 20 percent of the cyclists was on their cell phone. "Most of them listen to the radio or are talking on the phone. Only a few of them are actually typing, or holding the phone to their ear, but still, this constitutes sufficient distraction," says Director Peter van der Knaap.

English-Style

What they also noticed is that relatively many cyclists (5 percent) cycle in the wrong direction – also called 'English cycling', and that most of them (80 percent) do not look over their shoulder before making a move to pass another cyclist. This can cause serious accidents, the Association warns. These accidents have been registered by the cameras.

Widening

Van der Knaap indicates that serious measures are required. Such as widening the cycle paths on busy routes, so that also people who are using a cargo bike have a enough room to manoeuver. "If necessary, at the expense of parking spots," says the Association. This cycling behavior was studied during early morning rush hour in 2015. The Association says that it does not represent overall Dutch cycling behavior, but that it can be considered indicative of the behavior in other busy cities.

On average, a Dutchman cycles 2.5 km a day and 900 km per year

Bicycles, the Heart of Dutch Culture

by Jacob Vossestein

Ah, the bike, the Dutch bike, *de fiets*. Pity it wasn't invented in the Netherlands, for wouldn't it be a far better symbol of this nation than the tulip or the wooden shoe? It conjures up the very essence of Dutch culture, and I will tell you why.

Not all immigrants appreciate Dutch bikers, whichever background they may have. Foreign visitors find their behavior unpredictable, dangerous, and anarchistic – with bikers suddenly popping up when you least expect them. And I agree, it is all true, but let me take you along another line of thought which may be worth considering too…

To my idea, the Dutch bike – the simple, sturdy, run-of-the-mill

black bike, omnipresent in Dutch cities – reflects several traditional Dutch characteristics.

Obviously, in a flat and very crowded country, it is a pragmatic means of transportation that gets you everywhere in no time, certainly when you ignore traffic signs and other silly official obstructions which, as a tax-paying citizen, you may question and toss aside. In applying a riding style that foreigners tend to describe as 'suicidal', a Dutch city biker will reach his / her destination far sooner than when using the tram, let alone a car.

Another plus: everyone can afford a bike, be it new or second-hand. Not generally employed in any status games, it is a very egalitarian means of transportation. As bikers are exposed to rain and wind and the laws of gravity on steep bridges, any difference in status or social stature between them is soon eradicated, revealing the essence of life: a body struggling against the forces of nature. Office clerk, bricklayer, human resources manager or secretary of state, all bikers have to bow to the elements. And toiling against gale force 8 on an unsheltered dike road or a straight-as-a-ruler suburban street will encourage modesty in anyone, making him equal to his fellow human beings who suffer likewise. Well, theoretically, that is.

The bike also satisfies the Dutch inclination to not waste any resources. It is not only a cheap means of transportation, it also improves one's general shape, thus reducing medical expenses. On a slightly more abstract level, bikers can also congratulate themselves on the fact that their effort is for the good of the planet as a whole: no fumes, no noise, no use of exhaustible resources, no great amount of unnaturally paved space needed. What could be more satisfying than a good conscience combined with excellent health and a well-filled wallet?

But that is not all. Riding a bike could be seen as having a touch of philosophy to it, even spirituality. It teaches the rider balance, and we're not only talking about physical balance. Riding along during rush hour at about 20 km/h among scores of other bikers doing likewise, all – well, most of them – waiting for the red light to turn green, trying to find a clear section of road to cross, cycling through the pouring rain… Things like that produce a certain equilibrium with your fellow bikers, peace of mind almost, to quote a Hindu term. It makes you realize the true size of your ego: just a small flame among many, hardly more than that of a match, nothing special really.

Besides balance, biking teaches you alertness. Though the race may not be about winning, it's challenging nonetheless: avoiding the carefully parking truck, calculating whether you can still pass just in front of that car that has no right whatsoever to be going so fast, racing for a minute to catch the bridge just before it closes (or is it: opens?) for a ship, catching the orange light nanoseconds before it turns red and when this fails, scanning the surroundings for any signs of police presence.

So with eyes on all sides and ears open to the sounds of car tires, tram bells, moped noises and of course each other's ringing bells, bikers wind their way through the ever-changing river of traffic where they may physically be the weaker party but morally speaking are superior by far: unpretentious, silent, un-polluting, utterly democratic, going with the flow and yet self-willed. This feeling of modest self-righteousness gets stronger when the bike is used for the transportation of items such as the daily shopping, the two children, a dog, or a pile of wood for some do-it-yourself job.

There are a thousand and one subtle effects and conditions which become part of your delicate existence when you bike. In a densely populated nation, give and take are essential, and biking may be a good preparation for the bigger podium of life. Royalty, prime ministers and captains of industry have preceded you, so what's keeping you from joining the steel-framed army when going to work, school or the supermarket? If you can't beat us, join us. See you at the traffic light!

Some acts & Figures

▶ There are about 18 million bicycles in Holland, making that more than one for every inhabitant

▶ About 1.3 million new bicycles are sold every year

▶ The Dutch cycle approximately 13.5 billion kilometers per year

▶ The percentage of bicycle owners is the highest among those with the highest income

▶ There are 3,277 bicycle shops in Holland

▶ There are 19,100 kilometers of bicycle paths and lanes, and 116,500 kilometers of paved roads (including 2,235 kilometers of expressways)

▶ The Netherlands has one of the lowest car density percentages in the whole of the EU: 44.4%

▶ In the provinces of Drenthe and Noord-Brabant there are relatively more cars, due to the fact that distances are greater and public transportation not quite as omnipresent

▶ Conversely, the number of cars in the bigger cities is relatively low

▶ Almost 15% of the Dutch households have two or more cars, while fewer than one family in ten does not have a car

▶ Holland is the fourth safest country to drive in. Only the U.K., Sweden and Norway have lower numbers of fatalities

▶ There are 5,046 kilometers of waterways navigable for ships of 50 tons

▶ There are approximately 162,000 recreational boats in the Dutch harbors / water sports companies

▶ In Drenthe, there are a 1,000 recreational boats, in the provinces of North Holland and South Holland, there are 32,000 each

▶ There are 2,808 kilometers of standard gauge railways

▶ On average, the Dutch travel a little over 30 kilometers a day: 22.5 by car (either as a driver or a passenger), 3 by train and 2.5 by bike

▶ 8.6 of these kilometres are work-related, 6 are for social purposes (visiting other people's homes), and 5.5 for sports, hobbies or going out

Driver's License

As a rule, residents of the Netherlands are required to have a Dutch driver's license in order to drive a motor vehicle. You are a resident if you spend at least 185 days per calendar year in the Netherlands.

Here are a few additional rules (or, as the case may be, exceptions):

► If you have a driver's license that was issued before January 19, 2013 and that was issued in the countries listed in the box, you are entitled to drive in the Netherlands on your foreign license for ten years after it has been issued, unless it expires earlier, in which case you can use it until that date

► If your license is over nine years old and you have registered with a Dutch municipality, you can use it another two years as of the date of registration

► If your license was issued after January 19, 2013, you can use it for 15 years, provided it is still valid. After this period, you will have to get a Dutch driver's license – to which purpose you can exchange it. You can also opt to exchange it for a Dutch license straight away.

► If you have a driver's license that has been issued in any other country, you may drive in the Netherlands on your foreign license for a period of six months (185 days) after registering as a Dutch resident. During this period, you have to take a driving test in the Netherlands to acquire a Dutch driver's license

► If you had a Dutch driver's license that was valid after June 30, 1985, then in most cases you can exchange your foreign driver's license, no matter which country issued it, for a new Dutch license

► You cannot exchange a so-called international driver's license for a Dutch license, as it is merely considered to be a translation of the national driver's license.

Exchanging Your License

If you live in the Netherlands and have valid residential status you may trade in a valid driver's license issued by the countries listed in the box, as well as Aruba, Monaco, Isle of Man, Netherlands Antilles, and the State of Jersey for a Dutch license.

Driver's licenses issued in the following countries can be exchanged if they cover the categories listed here: Taiwan, B (passenger car); Israel, B (passenger car); Japan, IB (passenger cars and motorcycles of more than 400cc); Singapore, Class 2 (motorcycles of more than 400cc) and Class 3 (passenger car), Andorra (license for passenger cars); South Korea, second class ordinary license; the Quebec province of Canada, Class 5; and all categories of licenses from Aruba, Netherlands Antilles, Jersey, Isle of Man, and Monaco.

The procedure for exchanging your license can be found on the website listed below.

The 30%-ruling

If you are benefiting from the 30%-ruling, you and the other member(s) of your family can simply exchange your license, no matter where you are from. Ask for an exchange form for your foreign driver's license at your local municipal office.

License Verification

The Department of Road Transport may ask you to have the validity of your driver's license and the significance of certain information confirmed by the Consulate or Embassy of the country that issued the foreign driver's license. You may also be required to have the content of the foreign driver's license translated by an approved interpreter/translator. For Japanese, Taiwanese and Chinese licenses, this is obligatory.

Certificate of Fitness/Medical Check-Up

You need a Certificate of Fitness (Verklaring van Geschiktheid) to prove that you are medically fit enough (physically and mentally) to drive a car. In some cases, you may have to undergo medical examination. When, and how, to go about this, you can find on the website listen below.

Return of Your Original Driver's License

The original driver's license will be returned to the embassy or country of origin of the license. Depending on the legislation of the country that has issued the license, you can then have it returned to you.

Taking the Driver's Exam

If your driver's license cannot be traded in, you will have to take a theory test and a road test at the Central Road Aptitude Bureau (Centraal Bureau Rijvaardigheid, or CBR).

You can take the Theory Exam in English. It takes one hour and consists of 65 multiple choice questions, 40 of which test your knowledge of the Dutch traffic rules (a maximum of 5 mistakes is allowed) and 25 of which test your recognition of, and response to, dangerous situations in traffic (a maximum of 12 mistakes is allowed). Below we have listed two sites that can help you arrange driving lessons and the exam in English.

Websites

► General information: www.rdw.nl/englishinformation
► Driving lessons in English: www.dutchdriverslicense.com

Westerschelde Tunnel

Health
Care

Going to the Doctor

The GP

Ah yes... Your first sneeze. Your throat hurts. Time to go to the doctor... Or is it?

Beware: culture shock coming up! In the Netherlands, no one goes to the doctor for a cold. After all, with these wet and rainy winters that have everyone sniffling their way through the day – if they all went to the doctor, he wouldn't have any time left! Or so the Dutch think. In general, they believe in seeing if whatever they have goes away of its own accord. And even if it's serious enough to warrant a visit to the GP, chances are he'll send you home with the advice to take it easy and drink lots of fluids... They're not much into any type of medication and certainly not antibiotics. There are even ads on the radio, aimed at dissuading the general public from poppin' them pills too frequently, warning us against the consequences of using them willy nilly.

But say you decide you want to go to a GP. First, you have to find one, which you can do by asking around among your colleagues, neighbors and friends to see whom they recommend. The GP is someone you have to feel comfortable with when you are feeling at your least comfortable, so take your time and arrange to meet your new doctor, if that makes you feel more at ease.

Appointment

GPs have two types of appointment schedules: either one by which you call and make an appointment (usually for the same day, maybe the next) or they have *inloopspreekuur*, which means that the doors open at, say 8:00 A.M., and you can just walk in; first come, first serve. Expect your appointment to last not much longer than 10 minutes; if you think you'll want more time, ask for a double appointment. For non-office hour emergencies, you call your doctor's office and a voice recording will tell you whom to contact. Increasingly, this is a so-called *huisartsenpost* (GP office) at the nearest hospital. In most cases, emergencies that require stitching or a cast can be dealt with by your GP or the SEH (Spoedeisende Hulp, Emergency Help) at a hospital. Not all hospitals offer SEH anymore, so be sure to find out before you race over there!

For simple questions, or to request a refill for your prescription, most doctors have a *telefonisch spreekuur*, whereby you can call in and speak to the doctor (or, at times, his assistant, who has followed special training) with your question or request.

Seeing a Specialist

If you want to see a specialist, you can't just pick up the phone and call a hospital (which is from where most specialists work). You have to go to your GP first, and discuss your problem with him; ultimately, he will decide whether he thinks your problem is cause for referral. This sounds worse than it is; if you really want to see a specialist, just be adamant.

Next, make sure you hold on to the referral notice your GP gives you. Once you've made your appointment, you will have to show it to the specialist's assistant as without it, your insurance company will not cover the expenses. Your appointment will probably be canceled if you don't bring it. International insurance policies (rather than local Dutch ones) may have different rules regarding specialist referrals, so consult your specific policy to be sure of what to expect.

There might be a waiting list, and if you speak Dutch, you can look these up on the site listed below. Else, you can ask your GP or a local friend if they can help you find out more.

The specialist will read the note provided by your GP, discuss your situation with you, arrange the necessary tests and prescribe a possible treatment. Probably, you will not be filling out four pages of your own (and your entire family's) medical history before the visit – but this really depends on your medical problem. If there is anything potentially of importance, be sure to mention it – such as former illnesses, hereditary afflictions and allergies to medication.

First Visit

If this is your first visit to the hospital, you register at the front desk. There you will be asked a few questions (your name, address, insurer, GP, and a few other questions). This information will go into the computer and also onto a little credit card-sized plastic card, called a *ponsplaatje*, which you must bring with you every time you go to the hospital as it is used, among others, to find your records, mark forms, send your bills to your insurance company, and to print out labels for lab tests.

Some hospitals now make use of an electronic card, called the *electronische patiëntenpas*. Some hospitals have neither – so it is best to ask at the information desk the first time you go to the hospital.

For insurance coverage, check our item on *Insurance*

Medication

If your GP or specialist decides you will need medication, he will give you a prescription (*recept*). If you live in a country where you leave the doctor's office with a prescription for at least three types of medicine no matter what you have, then you had best be prepared. As mentioned earlier, when it comes to your standard afflictions, Dutch doctors have great confidence in your immune system's ability to deal with your unwanted invaders adequately. Of course, serious problems will be given serious attention and commensurate medication.

Prescription drugs are filled at an *apotheek* (pharmacy). They computerize your prescriptions and keep a close watch on the drugs you are taking in order to avoid drug interaction. Many bill your insurance company directly for the costs of prescription medicine.

Approximately 465 children are born every day, while 405 pass away

Alternative Medicine

Alternative medicine such as acupuncture and homeopathy are also very popular in the Netherlands. For more information, get in touch with the *Alternatieve Geneeswijzen Infolijn* (website provided below). Homeopathic medicines can be purchased at either a pharmacy, a drugstore, or a health food store, and are generally not covered.

If you need physical therapy, manual therapy, haptonomy, chiropractics, (psychological) therapy, cranial-sacral therapy, or need other help with physical disabilities, or need advice on your sexual health, ask your GP for recommendations – don't forget the referral notice!

Websites
▶ Waiting lists hospitals: www.zorgatlas.nl/thema-s/wachtlijsten/wachtlijsten-ziekenhuiszorg
▶ Alternative medicine: www.infolijn-ag.nl

Nine Truths and Myths About Pregnancy

There are many myths and legends surrounding pregnancy and child birth in the Netherlands. Here we deal with a number of them.

TRUTH or MYTH?
I will have to give birth at home.

Myth. Being the no-nonsense, medical-issues-are-merely-a-blip-on-the-road people they are, the Dutch definitely romanticize home births, stressing how at ease they will feel giving birth in their own bed/bathtub. Yet, not even 20 percent of births take place at home. You might have been told that only home births are covered by your insurance, but also that is not true. If you have a medical conditioning warranting hospital birth, your insurance will fully cover the birth in the hospital. Also, you can opt for a *poliklinische bevalling*, in which case you go to the hospital when your contractions reach a certain frequency and leave within hours of the baby's birth. Most insurance companies cover this too. You might have to pay a contribution. Home birth-related costs are indeed fully covered.

Not even 20 percent of the Dutch women give birth at home

TRUTH or MYTH?
I won't be able to go to a gynecologist; I will be treated by a midwife.

Myth. Most pregnant Dutch women go to a local midwife, who is also present when the baby is born. (Most midwifes share a practice. This means that you will not necessarily always see the same one on each visit and that the midwife who is on duty is the one who will be holding your hand when you give birth.) However, if you wish to go to a gynecologist, you can request this. Certainly if there are medical problems, you will be referred to one straight away. If the gynecologist deems this necessary, you will stay under their supervision.

If you have continuously been under midwife supervision, she will also be present should you decide to have your baby in the hospital. The advantage of the latter is that, now that you are in a hospital, a gynecologist will be close by in case of emergency.

TRUTH or MYTH?
I will have to give birth without painkillers.

Myth. You don't *have* to give birth without painkillers. Midwifes are generally not allowed to administer them, so if you give birth at home, you will have to make do without them – unless you try out acupuncture, TENS or hypnosis. If you give birth in the hospital, you have a variety of options: laughing gas, an epidural, remifentanil, and painkillers.

TRUTH or MYTH?
The midwife does not carry out any medical check-ups.

Truth. Here's what they *do* do. They listen to the baby's heart; they monitor the baby's position, the growth of your uterus, your blood pressure; and, if they can't carry this out themselves, they send you to a specialist to carry out an ultrasound during your first or second visit, to verify the pregnancy, your progress and the number of babies inside.

You visit a midwife once every four weeks, during the first half of your pregnancy. After that, the frequency of the visits increases. Your midwife becomes your friend, someone who takes her time for all your questions, concerns, doubts and hopes, and she will always refer you to a gynecologist if you, or they, need more answers or reassurance.

TRUTH or MYTH?
Someone will come help me out the week after I give birth.

Truth. This is called *kraamzorg* (maternity home care). The *kraamverzorgster* takes care of you and your baby and is a valuable source of information and reassurance who offers you practical tips on your recovery, the baby's development, nursing, bathing, safety when sleeping, pets, etc. Generally, she will make sure that you take care of yourself too, and will provide you with healthy food and time to take a nap.

You have a legal minimum right to a total of 24 hours of *kraamzorg*, spread over eight days, though your insurance policy may cover, for instance, 80 hours over a maximum of ten days.

TRUTH or MYTH?
There is no prenatal testing.

Myth. The Dutch medical system offers prenatal screening and prenatal diagnostics to those who want it. It is not obligatory. Prenatal screening includes: testing your blood group and checking for possible STDs; the Combination Test that tests for Down's Syndrome (a combination of a blood test and a neck fold measurement); the Triple Test (to check for Down's Syndrome); and an ul-

---

FERTILE STORKS

During the 17th century, there was no such thing as the sexual revolution. Babies and the conception thereof were shrouded in mystery. In order to answer such painful questions as 'Where do babies come from?' the Dutch came up with the following, absolutely plausible, explanation: babies were brought by the stork. If this failed to impress the children, other, equally plausible, explanations were available: babies were found among the beets, or they were found in wells or in hollow trees.

Why, of all birds, did the stork get to be the one to deliver this precious freight? In the Netherlands, storks were always considered harbingers of good luck. Therefore it was only logical that they would be the ones to bring proof of the fact that the mother was fertile, the marriage fruitful and the father a real man.

Nowadays, if you pass a front yard with a stork in it, you can be sure that this is the announcement of the birth of a new world citizen. The use of storks is also very popular on birth announcements.

---

trasound at 20 weeks' pregnancy. Prenatal diagnostics are offered to pregnant women at a reasonable price, and include Chorionic Villi Sampling (to check the chromosomes and DNA and test for genetic abnormalities); Amniocentesis (to tests for genetic abnormalities and the chances of Spina Bifida); additional ultrasounds; and NIPT (Non-Invasive Prenatal Test), to check for genetic abnormalities, and which can be used instead of Chorionic Villi Sampling or Amniocentesis.

TRUTH or MYTH?
I have a right to pregnancy leave.

Truth. If you are (self-)employed, have a right to 16 weeks' paid leave surrounding the birth of your baby, which can be initiated between 4–6 weeks prior to the estimated due date. In fact, *you may not work* from four weeks before, until six weeks after delivery (not that anyone will be checking this if you are self-employed). If the baby is late, and you have used up the six weeks beforehand, you also still have a right to a ten-week leave following the baby's birth.

During pregnancy leave you receive 100 percent of your normal wages – either directly from the Social Security Institution or via your employer – up to a maximum of the so-called daily wage a day, though some employers pay out the gap between this and your full last-earned salary. For self-employed moms, the amount you receive depends on the number of hours you worked in self-employment the previous year.

TRUTH or MYTH?
Daddies also get some time off.

Truth. Dads/partners are entitled to paid leave on the day the baby is born, and – starting in 2017 – five days of paid leave following the birth of their child to stand by the mother right after birth. They can use this time to register the birth of the baby (which has to take place within three working days after birth) at the *gemeentehuis* (town hall) in the city or town where the baby was born – not where the baby lives, unless this is the same.

TRUTH or MYTH?

I, or my husband, can take unpaid leave to take care of my children.

Truth. At some point during the first seven years of your child's life, both of you can take unpaid leave of absence to care for your child (adoption or foster child included). In principle, the idea is that you work 50 percent during a period of one year, but as the rules are not always practical – for either the employee or employer – other conditions may be agreed upon. Both of you can do this at once, or one after the other. In the case of twins, you can take twice the amount of leave. Although not required by law, some employers continue to pay up to 75 percent of the wages during parental leave.

Favorite Pets of the Dutch

aquarium fish

1

9.4 million

8.5 million

2 fishing pond

birds

cats

4

3 3.1 million

3.9 million

chickens, ducks and geese

dogs

6

5

1.5 million

2.2 million

8

9 rodents

rabbits

7

pigeons

600,000

1 million

900,000

10

250,000

reptiles and amphibians

The Dutch and Their Pets

Dog Tax

If you have been living in the Netherlands for a while, you have undoubtedly taken a slip over *hondenpoep* – dog poop. Rather than enjoying the beautiful architecture of the Dutch cities, you find yourself staring at the sidewalks, navigating your way around the deposits of our furry friends. How can it be that this nation of clean, hygienic, well-educated people can live with sidewalks pockmarked with *hondenpoep*? If we had an answer, we'd tell you. There is, however, an ongoing campaign to have dog owners train their dogs to leave their mess in the roadside gutters (watch out when stepping out of the car!) and dog owners pay taxes for their hounds.

This tax used to be a 'corporate' tax, but is now levied on private dog owners, the proceeds of which are used to create areas within the cities and towns that can be considered public dog toilets. This is the only pet-related tax there is, so maybe there is some justice after all.

Pet Care

Pets have a position in Dutch households that is very similar to that of the children. Some are served the best cut of the rarest beef, others are given the best chair, with the best view of the TV – and, naturally, access to the accompanying snacks. And the care provided is top-notch: the veterinary services (a vet is called a *dierenarts*) are excellent in the Netherlands, and include animal hospitals, ambulances and even crematoriums. There are also dog-walking services (*honden uitlaatservice*) for those who can't imagine life without Whoofy, but unfortunately have to spend the whole day in the office. And last but not least, the pet stores in the Netherlands offer a wonderful array of toys, cushions, cages, leashes, snacks, top-of-the-line food, and… pets, of course.

Finding a Pet

If you want to buy a dog, however, it is always better to do this via a recognized breeder rather than through a pet store. Breeders can be found through the Raad van Beheer op Kynologische Gebied in Nederland (www.houdenvanhonden.nl). For any other type of animal (other than the household rodent type – for which the pet store, or the petting farm, called *kinderboerderij*, will do fine) – you can best ask the local vet where you can find one. If you are looking to save an unwanted cat or dog, there are kennels, called *dierenasiel*, where 'lost and found' or otherwise homeless animals are brought. These kennels are well-run and most of the time have a good profile of the animals they are trying to place. Often, they have to find a new home for the pets of families who have to go abroad, or who have family member who is allergic to animals and find it greatly rewarding to have found such a loving pet a new home.

Notes

Colophon

ISBN 978 946319 014 5
NUR 530, 600

© 2016, XPat Scriptum Publishers

No part of this book may be reproduced or transmitted in any form
or by any means without permission from the publisher:

XPat Scriptum Publishers
Nieuwe Haven 151
3117 AA Schiedam
the Netherlands
Tel +31(0)10 427 10 22
E-mail info@xpat.nl / info@scriptum.nl

Editor
Stephanie Dijkstra, Across Borders Driebergen

Text
Stephanie Dijkstra, DutchNews.nl, Arnold Enklaar, Han van der Horst,
Annebet van Mameren, Ana McGinley, Molly Quell, Hanneke Sanou,
Jacob Vossestein

Design
Ad van der Kouwe, Manifesta Rotterdam

Photography
Alamy, Ben Deiman, Dreamstime, The Holland Handbook,
Iamsterdam, Kevin McPeake, Shutterstock, Karel Tomeï (aerial photography)

Print
DZS Grafik

Visit us at
www.xpat.nl
www.scriptum.nl

Insofar as possible, we have requested permission
from the rightful claimants to use the illustrations
and photographs contained in this book.
Anyone who is of the opinion that they have not
been approached on this matter while they feel they
should have, is requested to contact the publisher.